Smart Thinking

How to Think Big, Innovate and
Outperform Your Rivals

D1262607

Smart Thinking

How to Think Big, Innovate and
Outperform Your Rivals

ART MARKMAN

piatkus

PIATKUS

First published in the US in 2012 by Perigee, a division of Penguin Group, USA
First published in Great Britain in 2012 by Piatkus

A CIP catalogue record for this book
is available from the British Library.

Text design by Kristin del Rosario.

ISBN 978-0-7499-5768-1

Printed and Bound in India by
Gopsons Papers Ltd., Noida

Papers used by Piatkus are from well-managed forests
and other responsible sources.

Piatkus
An imprint of
Little, Brown Book Group
100 Victoria Embankment
London EC4Y 0DY

An Hachette UK Company
www.hachette.co.uk

www.piatkus.co.uk

For
Lucas, 'Eylam, and Niv.

CONTENTS

FOREWORD

In every walk of life, it is an advantage to be smart. The businesses that get out in front of the pack are usually the ones that outthink their competitors. The people who live long and vital lives are usually the ones who have consistently made smart choices.

The value of smart is obvious—it underlies our ability to think, reason, make decisions, communicate, and take action. That's why people are constantly searching for advice about how to think smarter and more effectively. And there's certainly no shortage of books on the subject.

Most of those books fall into one of two camps. There are many authors with beliefs and intuitions who want to tell you what has worked for them in the past. Their advice often has the feel of good common sense, but it isn't backed with any real science. There are also books written by scientists, which are heavy on the details, but light on practical recommendations.

Every once in a while, you find a book that combines leading-edge science with *news you can use*. Our friend and colleague Art Markman has written just such a book. As one of the world's most respected voices in the field of cognitive science, he has spent the last 20 years as a university professor writing papers for scientific journals and advancing what cognitive science knows about thinking. But, he has also spent time outside of the lab working on real problems. He works with companies to give their employees new ways to think. He even contributed some psychology background to two of the *You* books.

In *Smart Thinking*, Art has taken his command of cognitive science from his own research and from his experience as a journal editor and boiled the discipline down to its essence. He has isolated a formula for thinking more effectively. But, he doesn't just report the research, he gives it to you in a highly actionable form. The book is filled with specific suggestions and tips that you can use to create new habits to think better starting literally from Chapter 1.

So, whether you're a student just starting out, an executive looking for an edge in the business world, or someone who is curious about how an understanding of psychology can change your life, *Smart Thinking* has a lot to offer.

But remember, just as good health requires effort on your part to learn about your body, eat right, and develop a routine for exercise, Smart Thinking requires effort to learn about your mind, and to change your daily thinking habits. Reading this book, then, is an important step toward success.

—CRAIG B. WYNETT AND DR. MEHMET OZ

Craig B. Wynett is chief learning officer for the Procter & Gamble Company. Dr. Mehmet Oz is vice chair and professor of surgery at Columbia University, bestselling author, and Emmy Award–winning host of *The Dr. Oz Show*.

Smart Thinking

ONE

What Is Smart Thinking?

**Smart Thinking and intelligence
are not the same.**

Learn the formula for Smart Thinking.

Evaluate your own behavior.

WHEN I WAS IN HIGH SCHOOL, I WORKED CLEANING an office building on weekends. I emptied ashtrays and trash cans, scrubbed the kitchen and toilets, and vacuumed the carpets. I plugged in a loud industrial-strength vacuum and ran it over the floors. The big canvas bag at the back of the vacuum would inflate, and sometimes a fine stream of dust would flow out of the bag and into the air. I used to get home after cleaning and take a shower to get the thin layer of dust particles off my skin.

I didn't see that as an opportunity, though.

At about the same time, James Dyson was also unhappy with his vacuum. It would suck the dust from the floor and filter it through the bag. He noticed that the dust would clog the mesh of the bag, and the vacuum would get less efficient the longer he used it.

Dyson decided there must be a better way. He redesigned the vacuum. He used a cardboard tube to create a cyclone. The cyclone created centrifugal force. The dust particles were thrown outside the cyclone and could be collected in a container. This new design led to a revolution in the vacuum industry and created a company that consistently makes over $100 million in profits a year.

Smart, right?

In 1999, Fiona Fairhurst—a designer and former competitive swimmer—and her team at Speedo went looking for a way to improve the performance of swimsuits for elite athletes. The central problem for her group is that when a person swims, the water exerts a number of forces against the body. These forces are collectively called drag. If you pull your hand quickly through a full bathtub, you can feel the drag acting against your movement. The faster you try to pull your hand through the tub, the stronger the forces that push against the movement. The design team started with the premise that there had to be a way to develop a swimsuit fabric that would decrease the effects of drag on a swimmer's body.

Fairhurst and her team looked to the animal kingdom for inspiration. They noticed that sharks are an interesting case. Sharks swim very fast, though their bodies ought to create a lot of drag. After analyzing samples of sharkskin at the Natural History Museum in London, Fairhurst found that they had structures on the skin called denticles that act to keep water molecules from sticking to the shark's skin. That structure lessens the drag on the shark.

The team created a fabric that mimicked the denticles in sharkskin and then made full-body swimsuits from this material. This new suit had a dramatic impact on the sport of swimming. Soon after its introduction, world record times in swimming started to tumble.

Surely, many groups had tried to create sleeker and more efficient swimsuits. Why was Fairhurst the one who made that happen? How did Dyson create a revolutionary new design for a vacuum while I just got covered with dust? Can these examples of Smart Thinking be explained by what we commonly call *intelligence*?

Intelligence is defined as an inborn quality that determines how well you are going to be able to think. You may have taken an IQ test at some point. The sections of IQ tests make you do things with numbers, have you mentally fold pieces of paper to imagine what they would look like, and figure out what picture would come next in a series. Funny how intelligence tests end up asking you to do things that don't look anything like what you do out in the real world. Indeed, it is a core assumption of IQ tests that the things they measure are largely independent of your specific knowledge. And it is true that IQ tests measure a real psychological quality. Your score on an IQ test won't change much over the course of your life.

You probably know a number of people who "test well." These people get great scores on IQ tests, SATs, GREs, LSATs. Some of them are also quite successful. They have gone on into the world, achieved their goals, and changed the way people around them think. Others have not lived up to their potential. They never found a passion. Their test scores were the high points of their mental lives.

Take the case of Bill, a guy I knew in college. We weren't great friends, but we would stop and talk if we saw each other on the street between classes. He got good grades in high school. When he was preparing his college applications, he took the SAT one time and got a perfect score. He was a solid student in college. His grades were respectable. He was witty and had lots of friends.

But, none of his classes really excited him. I never heard him talk about a class with a sparkle in his eyes. By our junior year in college, I had developed a love of cognitive science, but he took a smattering of classes, none of which really grabbed him. I remember seeing him a few months before graduation. On a whim, he took another aptitude test at the end of college, the GRE. This test gets used for admission to graduate schools. He got another perfect score. A score like that could get him into the graduate school of his choice. Because he wasn't that excited by any particular topic, though, he decided to go into the working world. I hear from Bill every now and again. He put together a solid career tutoring high school students for their classes. As it turns out, his real aptitude was for test taking.

I suspect that if I could look at Bill's score on an IQ test, it would be off the chart. Whatever intelligence is, Bill has it. But, Bill is no Dyson. He has no major inventions to his credit. He has not succeeded to the point at which he is a household name. He has not applied his raw intelligence to new problems.

And it isn't just Bill. Tests like the SAT, GRE, and the LSAT and even IQ tests are poor predictors of success in college or in life. At best, there is a moderate relationship between scores on these tests and students' grades in school. That means that there are plenty of people who get great scores on tests of intelligence, but don't succeed. Others get so-so scores, but find a passion and do great things in science, math, business, music, and the arts.

You don't have to rely only on anecdotes here. Lewis Terman was a psychologist in the early 20th century who helped develop IQ tests. He was particularly interested in people with high scores on those tests, and he was convinced that a high IQ was an important predictor of people's success in life. To try to prove this point, he gave IQ tests to a large number of children. From this sample, he identified a group of children who scored highly and followed them for years. This group—called the Termites—were all certified geniuses. Some of the Termites really did grow up to have highly successful careers. But not everyone was a great success. Of all of the children who took the IQ tests that Terman administered, one—William Shockley—went on to win the Nobel Prize in physics for his work developing the transistor. However, Shockley's score on the IQ test was not high enough for him to be included in the group Terman studied. Shockley won the highest honor that can be given to a physicist, but he was no Termite.

Some researchers argue that intelligence isn't one thing, but instead it is many different things. They suggest that IQ tests are not good at predicting success because they do not measure the right forms of intelligence or the right combinations to predict how well people will do in real situations. But even that more nuanced way of thinking about intelligence falls short as an explanation of Smart Thinking. Measuring someone's IQ does not tell you whether he or she engages in Smart Thinking, because most of what we are talking about when we say that someone has done something smart is not measured by tests of intelligence. That's because IQ tests focus almost entirely on abstract reasoning abilities.

But the Smart Thinking that led to the cyclone vacuum and the Fastskin swimsuit had nothing to do with abstract reasoning. Smart Thinking is really about the content of what you know and how you use it. Synthesizing the results of my own research with that of other studies in cognitive science, I come to a very different description of what leads to innovative ideas.

Smart Thinking:
The Ability to Solve New Problems
Using Your Current Knowledge

Science shows clearly that Smart Thinking is not an innate quality. It is a skill that can be developed. That is, you are not born
with a particular capacity to do smart things. Each of the components of being smart is already part of your mental toolbox.

To see the difference between Smart Thinking and intelligence, let's think about chess. On the surface, you might think that
chess is a great example of the power of abstract thought. The
standard stereotype of chess players is that they are highly intel-
ligent people who occupy themselves by playing this complicated
game. Researchers in artificial intelligence (AI) have been at-
tracted to chess partly because it is a game with clear rules and so
it is well-suited to a computer and partly because it is seen as a
hallmark of intelligence. AI researchers figured that if they could
crack the problem of chess, they would really demonstrate that
computers are smart.

What makes the game of chess so difficult is that there are an
enormous number of possible moves. If you just start laying out
the possible moves of the game, there are millions of potential
configurations of pieces on the board after only three moves by
each player. When computers are taught to play chess, much of
what they do is abstract reasoning of the type that intelligence
tests examine. Chess computers search through the set of moves
that could be made starting from the current position on the
board. The computer simulates what a good opponent would do,

and follows the most promising leads. The computer is trying to look as far ahead in the game as possible. This strategy has been quite successful, and in 1997 IBM's Deep Blue computer beat the reigning world champion Garry Kasparov.

Psychologists have also been interested in chess and have studied how experts play. It turns out that experts play the game very differently from the way that computers do. Chess experts learn lots of sets of opening moves that often lead to advantageous board positions. They also learn lots of endgame groupings of pieces that signal when a game can be won by one side or the other. In the middle of games, world-class chess players learn to recognize patterns of pieces that suggest new moves to take. They may follow a few possibilities forward through several moves to see what might happen, but they are not doing the kind of systematic search of millions of possible moves that computers do.

This research shows that it is the content of what experts know rather than some abstract reasoning ability that affects the way they play chess. One interesting experiment on this topic looked at subtypes of expert chess players. I don't play chess very well, and so I always assumed that every chess master plays the game in about the same way. Actually, chess masters are like tennis players. Just like there are some tennis players who prefer to serve and volley while others like to hit ground strokes from the baseline, different chess masters develop their own styles of play. In this experiment, researchers compared one group that was skilled in a particular opening style called the French defense to a second group that was skilled in a style called the Sicilian defense. Experts in the French defense were much better at solving new chess problems that reflected the way the board would look starting with the French defense than starting with the Sicilian defense.

Those who generally played the Sicilian defense were better at Sicilian defense problems than French defense problems.

Even in chess, it's what you know that matters.

The way that someone becomes an expert is to spend a lot of time learning about openings, and endgames, and strategies for playing the middle part of the game. Years of work give people specific knowledge about chess that they can use to play the game at the highest level. That is, chess is a skill, not a talent. It can be learned.

Smart Thinking is like chess. Even though it may seem like Smart Thinking must be some kind of talent, it is really a skill.

LET'S GET BACK TO JAMES DYSON. HOW DID HE COME UP with the idea for his vacuum?

To start with, he knew a lot about how mechanical things work. He realized that the way a typical vacuum works is that it lifts the dirt off of a surface with suction (and perhaps a brush to loosen the dirt). The air and dirt get sucked into the bag, and the bag itself acts like a filter. As more dirt gets trapped in the bag, the holes in the filter are covered up, and the vacuum generates less suction, so it works less well.

A typical way to try to improve a product is to try to fix each of the components to make it work better. For example, someone might try to find a way to keep dirt from getting in the mesh of the bag so that the holes remain open. It is common for products to get more complicated over time as different designers try to improve the parts.

Dyson didn't work that way. He set out to find a completely different solution. His method was to try to improve the function of a vacuum by exploring possible improvements that came from products that were not vacuums. To succeed with that strategy, he had to think about what a vacuum is really trying to accomplish. Most people were focused on finding better ways to filter the dirt from the air sucked into the vacuum. But, Dyson realized that any method that would separate the dirt from the air would work, and that filtering is only one way to create that separation.

It turns out that this same problem is solved by sawmills. When a sawmill cuts logs into boards, it generates a lot of sawdust. The mills suck the sawdust away using an industrial cyclone. Air and sawdust are drawn into an inlet in the top of a large cone at high speed. The cone shape of the sawmill helps create a cyclone—a column of spinning air. The spinning motion of the air pushes the sawdust outward through centrifugal force and gravity pulls it down the cone. The air exits the top the cyclone, and the sawdust hugs the side of the cone until it drops into a hopper at the bottom.

Dyson re-created this design on a small scale inside a vacuum cleaner. It took many different tries for him to perfect a working vacuum based on this initial concept, but this general approach was the basis of his very smart idea.

As fascinating as this story is, though, there is no magic here. Because Dyson knew about the way a lot of things work, he had what psychologists call *causal knowledge*. He also understood that it is possible to apply causal knowledge from one area to another area. While most people do not see the similarities between vacuum cleaners and sawmills, Dyson smartly recognized that there were crucial ways in which sawmills were like vacuums. Finally, Dyson was persistent. He spent time learning about things like vacuums and sawmills. And even after he had the great idea to use the principle of the sawmill to design a vacuum, he spent years perfecting it until it was ready to be brought to market.

If you look carefully at all sorts of people who have achieved great things—the things we attribute to Smart Thinking—you'll see that there is no magic in any of their stories. As one example, Thomas Edison, who is credited with a host of inventions that have driven the modern world, had a vast store of knowledge about the inner workings of mechanical and electrical devices. He was able to solve difficult problems in part by bringing together a lot of that knowledge. When he was developing a practical light-bulb, he focused both on the problem of creating a filament that would glow for long periods of time and also on how electricity might be distributed to homes. Most people developing lightbulbs used small batteries in their workshops, and that affected their designs in ways that made them less practical.

Edison envisioned an electrical distribution system that was like the systems in many cities for pumping coal gas through neighborhoods and into homes for lamps and streetlights. Sending electricity over a distance required high voltage, and so Edison's electric light designs were constructed to work at high voltages. Edison succeeded in creating a practical design for the lightbulb because of the way he brought all of the parts of his knowledge together, including his understanding of electricity and of the way coal gas was distributed.

Smart Thinking does not have to lead to a world-changing invention. Take the story of Keith Koh. Keith wasn't widely acknowledged to be a genius like Dyson, Fairhurst, or Edison. He was just a regular guy with a business that made office supplies. In his factory, he had special lamps that provided a bright white light that allowed the workers to check the color of paint on the finished product carefully. Unfortunately, those lamps were very expensive. When the filament burned out on one of the lamps, Keith wanted to figure out a way to fix the lamps rather than having to buy new ones. Keith had some lasers in the factory, and decided to fix the filaments using them. To prevent the laser from breaking the delicate glass around the bulb, Keith shot small lasers from different directions at the broken part of the filament. The combination of the small beams aimed at the same spot allowed the filament to melt and reform as a whole. Each of the beams was too weak to melt the glass around the bulb. Keith learned that trick from a professor he had in college. When he first learned to do this, he had no idea that he would need it later when he was in business. By reusing knowledge in his factory, Keith was engaged in Smart Thinking.

WHY DON'T YOU KNOW ABOUT SMART THINKING ALREADY?

We live in what management guru Peter Drucker called the *knowledge economy*. The world prizes education, innovation, research, and expertise. Success in this world requires finding ways to be smarter.

Yet, you have probably never learned much about the way your mind works.

For that, you can blame the educational system. The structure of the science curriculum in the schools around the world has not changed much in over 100 years. Back when the basis for the modern science curriculum was being set up, there were long traditions in the scientific study of biology, chemistry, and physics. So, those sciences made the cut and became part of what every educated

citizen was expected to know. The scientific study of the mind—
psychology—was less than 50 years old at that point. It had just
split off from philosophy and was struggling to become a separate
discipline. In that era, it would not have made sense to try to teach
people what was known about psychology.

In the 21st century, though, psychology has learned a lot about
the way minds work. But because the agenda for your science curriculum got set over a century ago, you probably haven't been
exposed to much of that work. And that's a problem.

I love biology, chemistry, and physics. I would not want to see
them taken out of a general science education. It is important for
everyone to have an appreciation for the basic sciences, because
they have created the backbone for many of the technological innovations of the 20th and 21st centuries.

Realistically, though, most people will not have to apply the
specific knowledge they obtain about these basic sciences. Only a
fraction of the population will go into medicine or another field in
which a background in biology will be part of their daily lives.
Another small group will actually use a lot of the specific knowledge about chemical reactions and interactions among elements
that are the basis of a general chemistry education. Everyone will
obey the law of gravity, but only a few people will need the details
of their physics knowledge with any regularity.

Yet, every single person has a mind. Everyone who goes through
our educational system will be expected to use that mind to make
decisions, solve problems, interact with others, and communicate.
In fact, more and more people each year are taking jobs in which
they are expected to think for a living.

Even though everyone has a mind, we give almost nobody the
owner's manual. If you happen to take psychology courses in high

school or college, then you might get exposed to some rudimentary information about the way your mind works. If you choose to read some of the wonderful science books written for a popular audience, you might get some exposure to some of the secrets that the science of psychology has uncovered.

And though we can blame the educational system for why you haven't been exposed to much psychology so far, it is now up to you to fix that. Dyson didn't stumble on his design for a vacuum. Edison did not happen upon a good idea for a lightbulb. And you don't have to grope in the dark for the formula for being smart. Cognitive science knows a lot about how people use their knowledge to solve new problems.

The Formula for Smart Thinking

One day, one of my kids was doing a homework problem. He was staring at a simple circuit diagram that showed a battery connected to a resistor and a lightbulb. The particular question that had him stumped asked what would happen to the current in the circuit if the resistor were replaced with another that had more resistance. He hadn't been in class that day and had never studied electricity, and so he continued to stare at the diagram for several minutes without comprehension.

My son had reached what psychologists call an *impasse*, which is really just a fancy way of saying that he was stuck. One of the keys to good problem solving is to deal successfully with impasses. My son was not being successful. He sat sullenly at the table and his eyes started to glaze over. As luck would have it, I did know the answer to this question, because I had gotten a ham radio license as a kid and so I had to study some electrical theory. But, as a parent, I don't like to give my kids the answers, so I put on my best Socrates impression and went to work with him.

I asked him to describe the problem to me, but all he was able to do was to read it back to me almost word for word. I asked him what else he knew about electricity. He described to me how the electrons in a circuit flow from the negative part of the battery through the circuit to the positive part. I asked him what resistors did, and he said that they made it harder for the electrons to move through the circuit.

So, then I asked him if he knew anything else that flowed. He thought for a moment and then said that water flows. I told him to think about water flowing through a hose. I asked him to think about what it would be like for a water hose to have a resistor on it. He thought of bending the hose as he and his brothers sometimes do when I'm trying to water the plants or wash the car. He quickly realized that making the resistor bigger was like putting more of a bend in the hose, and so the flow of water would go down as the resistance went up. The frustration evaporated, and he went back to work. He solved the rest of the problems on the page by thinking about water hoses rather than electrical circuits.

In his own way, my son was doing the same thing that James Dyson did. He was using his existing knowledge to help him solve a new problem. Like Dyson, he was using knowledge that came from a different realm of expertise.

This example highlights two of the key elements of the general formula for Smart Thinking. It is crucial to *have High-Quality Knowledge* and to *find that knowledge when you need it*. My son reached an impasse because he could not find any knowledge that he had that was related to the problem. By suggesting ways to redescribe the problem, I helped him think of water flowing through a hose. Because he understood the way that water flow is affected by putting a kink in the hose, he was able to learn something new about the effects of resistance on an electrical current.

In this case, he was not able to access the knowledge he needed on his own. He had to have someone else's help to enable him to move forward with the problem. In general, an impasse feels so frustrating because you don't know what to do next. That feeling of being stuck makes you anxious. Getting anxious and stressed when trying to solve a problem is not usually a recipe for successful thinking.

Problem solving can be stressful in part because you have a lot of mental habits that you have generated through years of practice thinking. Unfortunately, not all of those mental habits are conducive to Smart Thinking.

The thinking habits you have are not part of some fixed mental tool kit that you were born with. Those habits were created by going to school for years and then they were reinforced by all of the thinking you have done since then. Smarter thinking requires developing new habits to complement the ones that have already brought you success. It also requires changing habits that are getting in the way of Smart Thinking. When you reach an impasse, you need to have habits that allow you to do for yourself what I helped my son do. You have to develop habits to create High-Quality Knowledge and habits to help you find it when you need it.

If we distill the examples of Dyson, Fairhurst, Edison, chess experts, and even my son, we get the formula for Smart Thinking:

SMART THINKING REQUIRES DEVELOPING SMART HABITS TO ACQUIRE HIGH-QUALITY KNOWLEDGE AND TO APPLY YOUR KNOWLEDGE TO ACHIEVE YOUR GOALS

There are lots of great demonstrations of the components of the formula for Smart Thinking in action.

A fine and well-known example of using Smart Habits to deal with an impasse comes from the world of product development: In the late 1960s, 3M chemist Spencer Silver was searching for a strong adhesive. It is not surprising that not all of the formulations he tried worked well. One in particular failed miserably. Rather than creating a strong bond between two surfaces, it balled up and became tacky. It would hold briefly, but objects that were stuck together could be pulled apart easily.

Silver had a sense that this adhesive might be useful for something, but he wasn't sure what. He was at an impasse. Rather than giving up, Silver made it a habit to mention the compound to colleagues whenever he had a chance.

At this point, Silver's colleague Art Fry entered the picture. Fry was one of the many people Silver told about his weak adhesive. Coincidentally, Fry was trying to solve a problem outside of work. He would place paper bookmarks in his hymnal but whenever he opened the book they would fall out. He didn't want to tape the bookmarks into place since that would damage the pages. With the information Fry got from his colleague, he tried putting some of the weak adhesive on strips of paper. It worked perfectly—holding the bookmark in place but without damage to the page. 3M introduced this product as the Post-It note in 1980, and it is hard now to imagine a world without them.

Another classic case of using High-Quality Knowledge comes

from an invention by George de Mestral, a Swiss engineer. De Mestral hadn't set out to make a discovery but when he would go hunting with his dog, cockleburs would stick to the animal's fur and de Mestral had to spend time picking the persistent seeds off the dog's fur and his own jacket. Rather than treating this ritual as an annoyance, de Mestral became curious about why they stuck to his dog's fur so insistently.

De Mestral examined some of the burrs under a microscope and discovered that they were full of tiny hooks. The dog's fur was unruly, and had lots of tangles and loops in it. When the hooks caught on a loop, they stuck there until they were pulled off.

De Mestral reasoned that if he could create something that had these hooks on it, then they would stick to any surface that had tiny loops. Working with some local textile experts, he devised a way to create synthetic hooks (burrs) and loops (dog fur). As he predicted, this pairing led to an easily reclosable connection, and so Velcro was born.

To see the role of Applying Knowledge from different domains, let's take the case of Mark McCormack. In college, McCormack was a pretty amazing golfer. He had the good fortune to play against future golfing legend Arnold Palmer, who was a student from a rival school. After his collegiate golf days, McCormack got a law degree, and his friend Palmer turned to him for legal advice.

At the time, athletes were not the constant presence in pop culture and advertising as they are today. But McCormack couldn't help but notice that professional athletes were similar to movie actors: They had adoring fans who wanted to meet them in person and, possibly, use the products they used. As a lawyer, he understood how agencies representing actors helped get endorsements and other perks for their clients. Using that model, McCormack was able to arrange for Arnold Palmer to play golf with heads of companies for a handsome fee and to get significant endorsements to connect his image with products just like actors often did. Before long, Palmer's income jumped. Other golfers soon signed on, and McCormack created IMG, the first major sports management agency.

McCormack himself had stumbled on the role of Applying Knowledge. His personal philosophy has been quoted as, "Be the best, learn the business, and expand by *applying what you already know*." In his case, by recognizing the similarities between athletes and movie stars, McCormack generated a whole new field.

Self-Knowledge:
The First Step to Smart Thinking

The central goal of this book is to give you the tools for smarter and more effective thinking. I first brought these insights together in a class I developed to teach executives at companies interested in enhancing the performance of their employees. By bringing these lessons to their employees, leaders are helping develop what I call a *Culture of Smart*.

To get started on the road to Smart Thinking, it's valuable to evaluate your behavior first. I often give the following quiz as part of my class to give everyone a chance to think through some of the behaviors related to Smart Thinking he or she engages in regularly. This questionnaire includes a set of behaviors that you may or may not perform. Put a check in the first box next to each item if you think this is something you *should* do. Put a check in the second box if you think this is something you *actually do*. Check both boxes if both categories are true.

Nobody is going to see this but you, so be honest with yourself.

BEHAVIOR	SHOULD DO	ACTUALLY DO
1. I often check my email on my smart-phone before and after meetings to keep up with what is happening.		
2. If I run a meeting, I limit the agenda to just a few items.		
3. I keep my email program running on my computer to try to deal with new issues right away.		
4. I have a few hours of my workday where I do not answer the phone.		
5. I routinely teach what I know to other people.		
6. When solving problems, I draw on examples from areas of work very different from my own.		
7. I usually take the same route to work every day.		
8. When I need to solve a difficult new problem, I find a few different ways to describe it.		
9. I treat each new problem in its own unique way.		
10. When I don't understand a point that someone has made in a meeting, I speak up and ask them to explain their reasoning.		

BEHAVIOR	SHOULD DO	ACTUALLY DO
11. I skim new articles in my field as a way to keep up with what is happening. I read them in more detail after I know they are relevant.		
12. I frequently talk to people about what they are working on.		
13. When I get stuck on a hard problem, I put it aside and move on to something else for a while.		
14. I draw lots of diagrams to help me understand problems.		
15. To be more productive, I multitask a lot.		

Before we go on, I want you to do one more thing. Some of the things on this list may have been actions that you were not entirely sure whether you should do. If you see any of those, circle them.

When you take a quiz such as this, you usually get a score that involves counting up correct and incorrect answers. Maybe after that, you get some general advice based on the number you got.

I want to evaluate the results in a different way. First, look at the two columns of boxes. If you checked the box on the left, did you also check the one on the right? Every time there is a check in one box but not the other, that means there is disconnect between what you think you should do and what you actually are doing. If there is something you believe you should do that you don't actually do, there might be a mental habit waiting to be formed. If there is something that you actually do that you believe you shouldn't do, then you may have a bad habit.

To help you interpret the results of this quiz, know that items

1, 3, 9, 11, and 15 are all things that you should avoid, because they get in the way of Smart Thinking. The rest are things you should be doing to promote Smart Thinking.

Was there anything on the list that you thought was good but wasn't (or the other way)? Was there anything on the list that you circled, because you weren't sure whether it was good or bad? Learning more psychology is going to help you know the right thing to do in those circumstances.

There is an important reason I gave you this quiz, and it is called the *illusory transparency effect*. To understand illusory transparency, I need to tell you a story:

> Long ago, a farmer was walking down the road. He looked dejected. He came across a peddler from a nearby village, and they stopped to talk. "Seamus," said the peddler, "you look awful. What's wrong?"
>
> Seamus said, "My crop has been dried out by the sun. My wife has taken ill. My eldest son broke his leg when our best horse escaped from the barn and ran off."
>
> "Ah," said the peddler, *"the goose hangs high."*
>
> "Aye," replied the farmer, "the goose hangs high."

You have probably never encountered the idiom "the goose hangs high" before, but chances are from the context you can figure out that it must mean something like, "things in life are pretty bad right now." Psychologist Boaz Keysar and his colleagues gave people stories like this one, and found that people were quite good at understanding new idioms.

Then the researchers asked people what they thought someone who had never seen the idiom before would think it meant. An idiom like "the goose hangs high" might seem to carry its meaning pretty obviously. Clearly, when a goose is hanging high, it is freshly killed, which is not good for the goose. So, it should be obvious to anyone who sees the idiom that it means that things are bad.

Except that Keysar and his colleagues gave another group of people a similar story. In this version, the farmer is happy, and he tells a good story about his thriving crops, healthy wife, and talented son. In this story, the peddler also responds with "the goose hangs high." Everyone given this story realizes that this idiom must mean that life is pretty good right now. They envision a situation in which a fresh goose has been killed for a feast, and so they assume that it should be obvious to everyone what this idiom means, even if they have never seen it before.

In each case, people are unable to imagine what it is like not to know what the idiom meant. They cannot approach the idiom with fresh eyes.

The same thing happens when you hear about Smart Thinking. Good advice about thinking is often advice that makes a lot of sense. Once you hear it, you can't imagine doing things any other way. That is true, even though you may have been doing things quite differently in the past.

Unfortunately, that often makes important advice about thinking sound as though it were common sense. It is easy to resist advice that sounds like common sense because the key to being smart shouldn't be something obvious.

By looking at your own behavior first, though, you'll realize that there are many ways that you do not follow the formula for Smart Thinking. By recognizing that situation now, you are creating a platform for changing your behavior and generating new and smarter habits. A crucial focus of this book is to help you recognize the bad habits you have that hold you back from Smart Thinking and to give you specific strategies that you can use to make deliberate changes to improve your effectiveness.

instantly smarter

Throughout the book, key concepts that you can use immediately to help you think and act more effectively will be highlighted in a box like this.

The Plan

In the chapters that follow, I present lessons that teach you about the three core aspects of thinking: Smart Habits, High-Quality Knowledge, and Applying Knowledge.

Chapter 2 explores the nature of habits. How are they formed? What factors allow you to develop new habits? How do you change old habits? How can you create habits that foster Smart Thinking? The definition of Smart Thinking involves using knowledge effectively. As I said earlier, being smart is more than just having potential, it is using that potential to accomplish something. We start with a discussion of habits, because you cannot succeed with Smart Thinking without creating Smart Habits.

To examine High-Quality Knowledge, it is important to understand the way your memory works and to learn how to improve the quality of what you know. Chapter 3 presents a core principle about limitations in what you remember, which I call the *Role of 3*.

We use this principle to better understand how to learn effectively and how to present new information effectively to others. Chapter 4 examines the way you learn about how the world works. This kind of *causal understanding* is central to your ability to solve new problems. For example, earlier in this chapter, I briefly described the way sawmills clean up sawdust. Did you read that description carefully or did you just gloss over it? Do you think you could explain how it works? If you just skimmed it, then you may have missed an opportunity to acquire knowledge about one particular way in which things work that might turn out to be useful in the future.

Finally, to improve your ability to Apply Knowledge, Chapter 5 delves into the psychology of similarity and analogy. Many of the examples in this chapter, including the stories of Dyson, Fairhurst, Edison, McCormack, and De Mestral, involve finding knowledge from one area of expertise and applying it to another. It is quite easy to see the similarities between domains like vacuum cleaners and sawmills when it is placed in front of you but quite difficult to think of it for yourself. Chapters 5 and 6 present strategies for creating problem descriptions designed to help you to find the relevant knowledge you need when you need it. These chapters all focus on the components of the formula for Smart Thinking. Chapter 7 brings these components together to show you how you can use them to solve problems and think innovatively.

Of course, it is one thing to improve your own thinking. Chances are, though, some of your most important thinking is done with other people as part of a larger organization or company. What can you do to promote Smart Thinking in the people around you? Chapter 8 provides specific suggestions to help you be a prime mover in creating a Culture of Smart.

I recommend that you take this book slowly. If I ask you to think about something for a few minutes, please do. Keep a paper and pen close by to take notes or to do simple exercises suggested here. Make sure that you read carefully. Explain things to yourself as you go along. (I'll address the value of explaining things to yourself in Chapter 4.) All the information you need for Smart Thinking is here. And I'm giving you tools and exercises to practice those new skills. The rest is up to you.

TWO

Creating Smart Habits
and Changing Behavior

The mind is designed to think
as little as possible.

Habits are created by consistent
mapping and repetition.

Habit change requires replacing
bad habits with good ones.

I'M TYPING THIS BOOK ON MY COMPUTER USING A
QWERTY keyboard. The name comes from the arrange-
ment of the first six letters on the top row keyboard. I learned to
type back in eighth grade. My mom thought it was important for
everyone to learn to touch-type, and so I dutifully signed up for
the class, sat behind a clanking mechanical typewriter, and typed
out "asdfjkl;" over and over, gradually adding other letters to the
mix until I could type without having to look at the keys.

I never thought much about the layout of the keyboard. That
was just how it was arranged. This layout isn't completely arbitrary, though. The modern QWERTY keyboard was developed by
Christopher Sholes to help in the development of mechanical
typewriters. Most early typewriters had metal bars with type at

the end of each that were smashed against the paper or a ribbon to print the character. If the typist pressed the keys for two adjacent bars too quickly, the bars would jam, and the typist would have to stop and clear them before continuing.

Sholes's design helped minimize how likely it would be for the bars to jam. Accounts vary about exactly what he was trying to accomplish. Some people suggest he was trying to slow down the rate of typing. Others believe that this arrangement kept people from typing letters housed on adjacent bars.

Whatever he was trying to do, he was not trying to maximize typing speed. In the 1870s, when mass-produced typewriters were first starting to appear, the idea of typing quickly was not an issue. It was amazing enough that the common person could create professional looking type.

So, while the QWERTY keyboard succeeds at keeping the bars on mechanical typewriters from jamming, it is not so good for promoting fast and effortless typing. Few of the most common letters in English are on the home row of the keyboard where you place your fingers as you start to type. Only one of the top six letters in frequency (*A*) is on the home row, and that one is typed by the left pinky, which is most people's weakest finger. Four of the common letters (*E, T, O,* and *I*) are on the top row, and another one (*N*) is on the bottom row. In addition, the arrangement of letters means that many words have to be typed using one hand, and many common letter combinations (like *UN, TR,* and *GR*) have to be typed with the same finger.

Over the years, people have developed keyboards that require fewer finger movements, that allow more words to be typed from the home row of the keyboard, and that allow typists to alternate back and forth between hands when typing. The most prominent of these keyboards is the Dvorak keyboard, invented by August Dvorak, an educational psychologist. He really did set out to design a keyboard to maximize typing speed. And his invention worked. In the 1930s, when it was common to hold contests among typists, those using the Dvorak keyboard layout often beat those using the QWERTY layout.

Despite the success of this design, few of us type on Dvorak keyboards. Instead, the QWERTY keyboard has remained the standard. The story of keyboards is a classic example of *path dependence*. A decision made early on for one reason (keeping keys from jamming) influences behavior long after that reason is irrelevant. After all, most of us type on computers that don't have bars that jam. In addition, there is software on most machines that will allow you to remap the keys on your keyboard to the letters they type so that the keyboard on your computer could be using the Dvorak layout starting today. But you probably won't change your keyboard layout to the more efficient Dvorak system— and you probably shouldn't.

There are lots of factors that contribute to path dependence, but I'm interested in just one here: habit. Even though the Dvorak layout might allow me to type faster than I do eventually, I have already developed habits for typing on the QWERTY keyboard. And this is a great habit to have. My handwriting is slow and impossible to read. But I can type fast enough to keep up with what I am thinking. So, being able to type without thinking about the letters is a good thing.

I am reminded of the value of this habit when I travel abroad. A few years ago, I was in Germany. The standard keyboard in Germany swaps the location of the Y and Z keys relative to the QWERTY keyboard. On a German keyboard, if you use the familiar movements and try to type the word "you," it will come out "zou." As a result, when using a colleague's computer in Germany, I had to stop every few words and retype. I found it difficult and frustrating to use the keyboard, because I had to start thinking about typing, when usually I can just think about what I want to say.

That is the essence of smart habits. The cognitive system is designed as much as possible *not* to think. There are lots of tasks that you do routinely that you don't want to think about. Habits allow you to turn those tasks into automatic routines so that you can focus your attention on more important things.

To get a feel for how widespread habit is in your life, think about a typical day. The alarm goes off. You wake up groggily and stumble to the bathroom. You brush your teeth, shower, make some coffee, and pack your things to leave the house. You drive to work, park, and walk through the halls to your desk. You fire up your computer and check your email for the first time during the day. It is barely 9:15 in the morning, and already your life has been dominated by habit.

Really?

Contrast this routine scene with your first morning in a hotel room on a business trip. The alarm goes off. You probably are not listening to a familiar radio station, and already things seem a little uncomfortable. You get out of bed, and you walk toward the bathroom. But, now you have to think about where you put your toothbrush. The shower has unfamiliar controls, and you spend a minute adjusting the temperature to get it right. You may have hung your clothes in the closet, but you feel like you have to double- and triple-check to make sure you haven't forgotten anything. On your way out of the room, you search for ten seconds to find the switch to shut the lights off in the room. You kick your foot into the door in a panic worried that you might have left the card key to the room on a desk.

Then you get in a rental car. It is drizzling, and you spend a minute searching for the lever to turn on the wipers and then adjusting them for the light rainfall. You drive slowly from the hotel to the office where you are going to work for the day, checking the street signs carefully to make sure you don't miss a turn. The signs in front of the office building are hard to read, and it isn't clear where guests are supposed to park, so you ask someone in the lot. When you get into the building, you have no idea where to go, so you check in with the receptionist and wait in the lobby. After a few minutes, someone comes by and leads you to the room where you will have your first meeting.

It is barely 9:15 in the morning, and you're mentally exhausted.

The difference between these two situations is habit. Your mind is designed so that it thinks as little as possible. Whenever there is a routine that you do in the same way all the time, you develop a habit for it so that you don't have to think about it explicitly any more.

At home, you know where to reach for your toothbrush in the bathroom. You have a particular order for the routine you use to wash up in the morning. You can operate all of the features of your car without giving them a second thought. You take a similar route to work each day, changing it only if there is traffic or an accident. You know all of the twists and turns to get to your office.

These are Smart Habits. You don't want to think about all of the details about how to go about your daily life. When you are forced to think about these details (say, when you are traveling to a new place or have moved to a new home) it is stressful and tiring. Life is better when you don't have to think specifically about how to do the most trivial and repetitive tasks.

Smart Habits enable you to perform *desirable* behaviors *automatically*. Automatic behaviors are ones that you do not have to think about consciously to perform. When you drive a car, you do not think explicitly about pressing your foot on the accelerator or engaging the signal in preparation for making a turn. In fact, if I asked you immediately after you made a turn whether you used your turn signal, you might not know for sure. You would probably assume that you had done so because you usually do. But you might not remember for certain.

Chances are, you have experienced this lack of memory for automatic actions before. Every once in a while you may experience a moment of apprehension that you have forgotten to lock the door of your house. Usually, even when you have this feeling, the door really is locked. Your uncertainty reflects that you have a habitual routine for leaving the house, and locking the door is part of that. Because you do that behavior automatically, you probably have no memory at all of locking the door, particularly if you are thinking about something else on the way out of the house.

I have trouble remembering whether I have closed the garage door when I get into the house. I usually press the button for the garage door opener after I park my car. But I'm often thinking about something else at the time. For a long time after moving into my house, I would have to pop my head back into the garage to make sure the garage door was closed. After years of these checks, I finally had a window installed in that door so that I no longer have to open it to see for sure whether I did in fact close the garage.

This introduction to habits has two key lessons. First, the key signature of a habit is that it is an action you can perform automatically without having to think about it consciously. Second, most of the time, your habits are Smart Habits. It is unfortunate that we often use the word *habit* to refer to behaviors that you want to change. Without habits, our lives would be a frustrating daily focus on the most basic tasks of life. Habits are a crucial part of Smart Thinking.

The Formula for Smart Habits

Just as there is a formula for Smart Thinking, there is a formula for Smart Habits, which requires only two ingredients:

- Mapping between an action and the environment consistently
- Performing that action repeatedly

Let's start with the first component of habit formation: *consistent mapping*—making a connection—between the environment and a behavior, which requires that there be some unvarying element that reliably signals the action that is to be performed. The *environment*, for our purposes, consists of both the outside world and your internal mental environment—that is, your goals, feelings, and thoughts.

A few examples may help here.

Let's go back to the QWERTY keyboard: Because each letter is assigned a particular key, whenever you want to type a letter—*T*, for example—you press the same button. In addition, when you learn to type, you begin by placing your hands in the same initial position, with your index fingers on the *F* and *J* keys. For typing, the outside environment consists of the keyboard. The internal mental environment is the goal to type the letter *T*. The action to be taken in this case is to move the index finger of your left hand up and to the left and to press the *T* key.

There are many similar cases of consistent mappings that are set up by the design of the objects in the environment. The accelerator and brake pedals on a car form a consistent mapping. Musical instruments are created to allow consistent mappings. The notes on a piano are always in the same order, and pressing a particular key always creates the same sound. Light switches are designed so that pushing them up turns on the light and pulling them down turns off the light.

Consistent mappings can also involve consistency in conceptual mappings. Basic arithmetic facts create a consistent mapping. When you have the goal to add two numbers, and those numbers are 1 and 4, then the answer is always 5. It does not matter whether you are reading the numbers, hearing the numbers, or thinking about them. The sum is always the same. As a result, you can create habits for basic arithmetic facts.

The action associated with a consistent mapping can be the activation of a goal that frequently occurs in that situation. When you take your familiar route home from work, there may be a particular intersection where you make a left turn. Driving home on a typical day, when you see that intersection, you automatically engage in behaviors that are associated with turning left (like using the turn signal and looking at the oncoming traffic). However, suppose someone has dropped a bag in the road in the left-turn lane at the intersection. Now, you can't automatically pull into that lane as you normally do. You still find a way to turn left, though. You just have to think a bit about how to drive around the bag. So, the goal to turn left was engaged automatically, but you had to think about how to perform the actions that allowed you to satisfy that goal.

There are many situations that may become strongly associated with goals. Habitual smokers tend to smoke a cigarette when they drink coffee. As a result, drinking or smelling coffee (or sometimes even talking about it) can create the need to smoke. Classrooms are associated with sitting and listening to a teacher. When people go into a classroom, they often sit down and face forward waiting for someone to talk. Recently, I went to back-to-school night at one of my kids' schools. The parents all filed into the classroom, sat at a desk, and looked expectantly toward the front of the room waiting for the teacher to start talking. Most of these parents haven't been students in school for years, but the habits from their school years are still there.

The second component of habit formation is *repetition*: Any time there is a consistent mapping between the environment and an action, and the action is repeated in that environment, a habit will form.

Sometimes you structure your life to get that repetition. In that case, you call the repetition *practice*. A musician practices scales or patterns to develop habits for playing them. A teenager practices driving to develop habits for pressing the accelerator and brake, using the turn signal, and identifying patterns of traffic flow. Children practice their arithmetic tables to develop a habit for producing the correct answer to basic problems.

Even without setting up a practice session, repetitions of a be-havior in an environment will lead to a habit. You probably do not go out of your way to practice your route home from work. Nonetheless, the repetition of the drive home over many days leads to a habit. Likewise, you do not practice using your email system, but quickly you develop habits for checking your email. You know automatically how to look at your inbox or where to find the button to reply to an email, and how to search for old emails.

Why does repetition create a habit? Psychologist Gordon Logan has argued that creating a habit involves shifting from *effortful thinking* to retrieving the correct action directly from memory. When you first learn to drive a car, you may have to think about pressing down the turn signal every time you want to make a turn. Each time that you have the goal to make a turn and you press the turn signal, however, a memory is stored away that associates the desire to turn with the action of pressing the turn signal. When you get enough of those memories in your system, it becomes faster to retrieve the correct action from memory than to think about it. At that point, the action happens automatically, and a habit is born.

How many memories is enough to create a habit? There is no hard-and-fast number. Perhaps the most important factor that affects the length of time it takes for a behavior to become a habit is the distinctiveness of the memory that is going to drive the behavior. It is easy to remember the details of your one trip to a vacation spot like Disney World, because there is nothing else in your memory to compete with it. It is probably hard for you to remember exactly where you parked your car in the office parking lot, though, because you have parked in the lot hundreds (or thousands) of times and every spot in the lot looks more or less like every other spot. All of these memories of places where you have parked your car will compete with each other when you try to call one to mind.

Similarly, you are faster to create a habit when the situation in which you will perform the action is unique. When there are many different actions that might have to be performed in similar situations, then the habit will take longer to pick up.

Let's contrast two cases. First, imagine you have moved to a new town. There is an intersection on your route from your office to your new house where you have to make a left turn. That intersection has an interesting church on one corner, and a restaurant on another corner. These two buildings provide unique landmarks. In this case, it will be relatively easy for you to retrieve a memory of what to do at the intersection on your drive home, and so it will quickly become a habit. After driving toward your new home only a few times, you'll be preparing to make a left at that corner without thinking about it.

Now, think about the amount of time you had to spend creating habits for your basic addition facts. Chances are, when you were in second grade (or so), it took you hours of practice over several weeks of your life to learn your addition tables. You may have drilled and practiced these facts both in class and at home with flash cards and worksheets.

Why is it hard to create a habit for addition? The difficulty arises because the individual arithmetic facts are not that distinctive. The facts are not distinctive because there are many facts that involve each number. The problem 2 + 4 requires a different answer from 2 + 7, even though both involve the number 2 and the operation of addition.

When you are learning to do addition, the two procedures you have for adding compete with each other. One of those procedures requires some effort. You start with the bigger number and then count up. Adding two and four means starting with four and then counting to five and six. The other procedure is effortless. You try to remember the answer. If you finish counting before you pull up an answer from memory, then the counting procedure wins. If you are confident you have pulled up the right answer from memory before you finish counting, then the habit wins.

After you solve the problem (by either method), you store another memory that 2 + 4 = 6. So, each attempt at an addition problem provides memories that will make it faster for you to remember the correct answer in the future.

The difficulty with math is there are lots of similar facts. You are learning 2 + 4 = 6, but at the same time, you are also encountering problems like 2 + 7 = 9 and 2 + 5 = 7. Sometimes, when you see 2 + 4, you will also recall some of those similar problems. When you retrieve these conflicting answers, you are going to be uncertain about which answer is correct. So you will finish carrying out your counting procedure before you have an answer from memory.

Once you have a lot of examples of addition problems in your memory, most of what you pull out of memory when you see 2 + 4 will be other situations in which you also saw 2 + 4. At that point, you retrieve information from memory faster than you can count, and so you have a habit.

Of course, in the case of math it gets even worse. As soon as you have learned a few addition facts, the teachers add more. Next you learn subtraction, and after that multiplication and division. The same numbers are involved in lots of these facts. And for addition and multiplication, the same two numbers require different answers depending on the operation. In the end, it requires a lot of memories to create a smart habit for math.

How can you tell that you have developed a habit?

One sign of a habit is that you won't think about the process of doing the behavior any more. When you do basic addition now, the answer probably pops into your head without any effort. When you drive a car, you don't spend time thinking about how to press the accelerator or tap the brake. When you walk into your bedroom, you neatly flick the light switch in an upward direction without even looking at it.

Another way that you can tell you have a habit is that you will have trouble in situations where the environment has changed in ways that no longer support your habit. In 2002, the Psychology Department at the University of Texas at which I work moved to a brand-new building. We were very excited about this move. We have a large department, and our faculty and labs had been spread across five different buildings on campus. After we moved, though, I noticed that a lot of my colleagues were looking a bit more frazzled than usual. Each of us was suffering from a disruption of our Smart Habits. In my new office, I had to move my garbage can and recycling bin. I would find myself with a crumpled piece of paper in my hand unsure of where to throw it away. Whatever train of thought I had going would depart long before I figured out where to dispose of the paper. Similar disruptions of thinking happened while searching for light switches, seeking pens, and other mundane aspects of daily life. As we all gradually settled into our new space, I think all of the psychology faculty at the University of Texas had a greater appreciation of the benefits of Smart Habits.

instantly smarter

Get a Good Night's Sleep

You spend about a third of your life asleep. That means that when you reach the age of 45, you have slept for about 15 years. You had better be doing something useful with all of that time.

Psychologists have known for a long time that sleep is important for your well-being. People who do not sleep enough have difficulty dealing with stress. They are irritable. They also have trouble sustaining attention.

Sleep also influences your ability to learn new things and develop new habits. While you are awake you have many different experiences. While you are asleep, brain processes help you integrate those new experiences into your memory in ways that make you more effective in the future.

Sleep helps in learning habits. If you are learning to throw darts, you might spend 30 minutes practicing hitting the *20* on the dartboard. That practice will help you improve your skill. Similarly, practicing the procedures for entering expenses into an accounting system will help you develop skills with a new piece of software.

Over the course of a practice session, you will see some improvement. As it turns out, though, you'll improve even more by getting a good night's sleep.

Why?

There are many different stages of sleep. The stage of sleep that is most familiar to people is rapid eye movement (REM) sleep. In addition, there are four stages of non-REM sleep. Each of these stages show different patterns of electrical activity when monitored using an electroencephalograph (EEG).

Research on the relationship between sleep and learning shows that different kinds of learning are associated with different stages of sleep. Some stages of sleep are good for learning habits, whereas other stages are good for learning new facts or relationships among facts. So, it is important to make sure you are going through *all* of the stages of sleep during the night. In addition, there are actually some kinds of learning that benefit most from the sleep you get toward the end of your sleep cycle. If you do not get a good night's sleep, then you will ultimately be less effective at learning and less effective at developing habits. To maximize the effects of your practice, get your sleep.

Using Your Smart Habits Effectively

From our discussion so far, there are two aspects of habits that promote Smart Thinking:

- The behaviors you perform habitually do not take up your precious cognitive resources.
- You do not have to create habits intentionally. They develop whenever there is a consistent mapping between your mental and physical environment and the behavior you want to carry out.

Knowing these principles can help you strive to create habits to help you eliminate distractions. It is particularly important to create good habits in your work environment or whenever you have to think deeply. Keep your workspace organized so that you can always find things you need in the same place. Choose one location for your pens and pencils so that you do not have to search for them. Pick a place for the garbage can and recycling bin and leave them there. The paper clips, stapler, and tape dispensers should not be moved around. When you need to find these objects, you do not want to have to devote mental energy to finding them. Thinking about where to find a pen will crowd out the thoughts you are trying to have about your work. If you create habits for finding basic objects, you can focus your thinking on topics that require your mental energies.

In general, you should be on the lookout for distracting elements of your daily routine. I often use sticky notes. I use them for bookmarks when I am reading. I write notes to myself that I hang on my computer monitor. I put them on my computer keyboard in the morning to remind me of things that I have to do before I start checking my email for the day. At some point, I noticed that I did not have one place where I kept my stack of sticky notepads. As a result, I would find myself interrupting my reading or thinking to search for a pad of notes. After realizing what I was doing, I found a place under my computer monitor where I could keep a pad. By creating this consistent mapping, I was able to streamline another portion of my day.

It is also essential to take the time to understand the basic habits that are important for any area in which you want to develop expertise. When I was about 35, I decided to learn to play the saxophone. I had played the piano as a kid, and I wanted to learn a new musical instrument. In particular, I wanted to learn to play jazz. I spent the first few months just working on getting a noise out of the instrument that sounded vaguely like a saxophone. Early on, I learned a few patterns that could be played over particular chords. But I resisted learning all of my scales, which just seemed like a lot of work. My teacher let me get away with that for a while, but eventually, it became clear to me that I would have to break down and practice them. It took a lot of time, and it was not always enjoyable. But it really was important. I simply couldn't play anything interesting if I was struggling to remember what notes could be played in a particular key.

And herein lies the fundamental problem in acquiring good habits. As kids, we bristle at the time it takes to learn things like the multiplication tables or the dates of historical events or the structure of the periodic table. But as kids there were teachers and parents and tests to force us to do the things that weren't any fun.

When you get older, it is hard to get motivated to put in the practice to create new habits. It would be great to skip all those repetitions and get on to the interesting issues. In situations like this, I'm often reminded of the movie *The Matrix*. In one scene, the main character, Neo, needs to learn to fight. Since his brain is connected to a powerful computer, with a few keystrokes by the computer operator, a program is downloaded directly to his brain. After a few moments with his eyes closed, Neo looks up at the camera with a smile and says, "I know kung fu!"

Unfortunately, that just won't work for the rest of us. There is no shortcut to habit formation. You have to bear down and get those instances into your memory. If you don't acquire the basic habits in an area, you won't become an expert. Smart Habits are not merely recommended for Smart Thinking, they are central to it.

When Good Habits Go Bad

Most habits are probably good when they are first formed. That is, for many of the habits that you do not create intentionally, there must have been some value to performing that particular behavior. That value is what causes you to repeat the behavior often enough to create the habit.

When I was a kid, I used to bite my fingernails. It became a habit that was ultimately very hard to break. However, when I started doing it, it must have felt good or relieved stress or at least it must have made my nails shorter. I did it often enough that it was hard to catch myself doing it. Eventually, there was a downside to biting my nails. My fingernails looked bad. And so, I had to break the habit.

Some habits become bad, because a behavior that has rewarding elements to it at one time also has negative consequences that may not have been obvious when the habit began. Overeating is one such habit. You may know conceptually that eating too much is a problem. But when you actually overeat, there are few really negative consequences in the moment. I suppose if you eat way too much, you may feel a bit queasy, but the world does not end. You don't become violently ill. Most of the time, you just enjoy the meal and then feel a bit full. And so you do it again . . . and again . . . and again. If you start doing this when you are young, it may not even have that many negative consequences. Eventually, though, if you take in more calories than you burn off, you'll start to gain weight. By the time you really notice that you have gained weight, though, your habit of eating too much is deeply ingrained.

Changing Habits

Not all habit change is driven by a behavior that has negative consequences. Sometimes the environment changes in some way, and a behavior that worked well in the past is no longer effective.

A few years ago, I bought a car that had a smart key. With this car, instead of getting in, inserting the key into the steering column and turning, I had to insert the key into a slot on the dashboard and press a button. The habit I had developed from more than 20 years of driving suddenly did not work at all. I would sit down in the car, key in hand, and find myself reaching to put the key in the steering column. At that point, I had to think about what to do next. It wasn't that the habits I had developed were bad, they just weren't relevant in the new environment. Unfortunately, being in a car and wanting to start it was enough to call the old habitual behavior to mind.

There are two important elements to changing habits. First, the presence of the old habit pushes you toward an action. Somehow, you must prevent the old behavior from occurring. Second, you have to replace the old habit with a new one, which requires storing new memories that associate the environment with new actions.

Habits are driven by your mental and physical environment. Whenever you are in an environment in which you usually carry out the habitual behavior, you are going to be put in a mental state to carry out that behavior again. That mental state consists both of the activation of the goal to perform the behavior as well as the preparation of the actions to perform it. When you have a goal to do something and that goal is currently trying to influence your behavior, then psychologists say that the goal is *active*. The strength with which that goal is trying to affect your behavior is its level of *activation*.

In most situations, you are not aware of either the activation of the goal to perform an action or the preparation of the actions needed to achieve the goal. If you are driving home from work using your normal route and you reach a key intersection where you have to turn left, the goal to turn left is activated. You prepare and execute the movements to engage the turn signal, and make the turn. You can do all of this without having to think about it consciously.

Suppose, though, that you need to stop to buy milk on the way home. To get to the grocery store, you have to continue straight at that intersection and go a few more blocks. When you reach that intersection, your habits will activate the goal to turn left. To stop yourself from making that turn, you have to engage conscious effort to stop yourself from carrying out the habitual action.

That conscious effort involves the frontal lobes of your brain, a key function of which is to stop or *inhibit* actions.

In the case of driving home from work, you will be successful at buying milk if you inhibit the action of taking a left turn and re-place it with the action of driving to the store. Unfortunately, inhib-iting habitual actions is effortful. Because it takes effort to stop an action, you will continue with your habitual action if you get dis-tracted. If there is an interesting story on the radio, you may become engrossed in listening to the story. When you reach the intersection where you have to go straight, you will not engage the systems that inhibit your habit, because you are devoting those resources to the story on the radio. Later, when you arrive home, you will realize that you have forgotten the milk.

Your ability to inhibit habits is also disrupted by stress, by long periods of self-control, and by the continued influence of your environment on your behavior. It is a common observation that people who are on a diet have difficulty sticking to their diet if they are having a bad day. There is a great running joke in the movie *Airplane*, a classic spoof of disaster movies. In the movie, the pilots of a plane get sick, and a commander on the ground has to figure out how to help one of the passengers land the plane. Over the course of the movie, this poor commander breaks a diet, starts smoking again, and ultimately reengages a habit of sniffing glue. For everyone, in the movies and in real life, stress impairs the functioning of the frontal lobes and makes it hard to stop habitual actions.

Under other circumstances you may find that you exhaust your capacity to control a habitual behavior if you have to expend mental and/or physical energy to prevent yourself from acting badly. Eventually you sap the strength to continue regulating yourself in what psychologist and author of *Willpower: The Rediscovery of Human's Greatest Strength*, Roy Baumeister and his research collaborators, refer to as *ego depletion*.

Consider, for example, the manager who may be trying to quit smoking. After a couple of weeks of success, he has a day in which an employee has angered him through carelessness at his job. Although they interact regularly throughout the day, the manager works hard to avoid creating a scene by reprimanding him publicly. At the end of the day, the manager finds himself pulling into the local convenience store to buy a pack of cigarettes because he just doesn't have the capacity to fight the desire to smoke that day.

In essence, the worst way to try to stop a habit is through what we usually call *willpower*. You can stop yourself from a bad habit sometimes, but you can't rely on willpower as the only way to break a habit.

Finally, the *environment* that suggests the habitual behavior can activate the goal associated with that action. As a result, even if you successfully inhibit the action, the goal will still be available to affect your behavior. If you are trying to lose weight, you may try to eat less food. Perhaps you have a habit to have a bowl of potato chips in the evening. When the evening comes, the time of day, and your familiar evening activities activate the goal of eating chips. Although you may stop yourself from eating the chips on one occasion, the goal to eat a snack is still active. At that point, you may start feeling cravings to eat. Cravings happen when you have an active goal that has been blocked. Cravings are your mind's way of reminding you that there is something you have left to do.

To stop an old behavior, then, you must not only prevent the habitual behavior from being performed but also deal with the goal that is activated by the situation.

EFFECTIVE WAYS TO BREAK A HABIT

You can help block habitual actions by changing the environment in ways that decrease the chances that the habitual behavior will be recalled. If you have a favorite restaurant where you overeat, then one way to keep yourself from overeating is to stop going to that restaurant. If the restaurant triggers the behavior, then avoiding the restaurant will make it less likely that this behavior will be retrieved from memory.

Of course, there will be times that you cannot change your environment. If you are trying to develop new eating habits and you often overeat in your own kitchen, then it is unreasonable to expect that you will stay out of the kitchen. In a situation like this, you want to disrupt your habits by affecting the consistent mapping from the environment to behavior so that your behavior can no longer be carried out automatically.

One way to make an action difficult to perform automatically is to remove things from your environment that would help you to carry out a behavior without thinking. If you often eat potato chips while watching television, stop buying potato chips. If they are not in the house, you will not be able to eat them mindlessly.

A second way to block habitual actions is to disrupt the specific actions that make up the habit. Earlier in this chapter I described the difficulty of waking up in an unfamiliar hotel room. This disruption, which is so frustrating when you are traveling, can be put to your advantage when trying to change habits. Move your dishes around the kitchen. Put the pots and pans in a different location. Rearrange the food in your refrigerator. Start shopping at a new supermarket, so that you have to really think about all of your purchases. Now, you will have to think about all of the behaviors in your kitchen that used to be habitual. Because you are in a position to think about these behaviors, you are engaging the systems in the frontal lobes of your brain that can also be used to stop you from carrying out your habit.

The point of these recommendations is to put you in the best position possible to create a new habit. Avoiding situations that trigger a habit will make it less likely that you will perform the habit you want to change. When you disrupt your environment, you create a situation that is like my new car with a smart key. The habits you have developed are no longer applicable. You are now forced to be mindful about your behavior.

REPLACING OLD HABITS WITH NEW

So far, so good. You have given yourself the best possible chance to avoid performing the mindless behaviors that sustain your bad habit. Now, you need to reprogram yourself with a new habit to replace the old one.

Perhaps the most important insight about habits is that they are created by storing lots of instances of a behavior in memory. This is where it would be nice if you could just find those memories and remove them the way you might delete an unwanted document from a computer. Unfortunately, your mind doesn't work like that. You can't just erase things from memory at will.

In fact, the best way to disrupt a memory is to interfere with it. In the case of habits, that means creating new memories that are similar to the old ones. You have to associate new habits with each environment in which you used to perform the habitual behavior.

This point is an important one. Many of the hardest habits to break are ones in which you are trying to replace *something* (a behavior) with *nothing* (the absence of the behavior). People who want to quit smoking typically think of this change as stopping an undesired behavior (smoking) and replacing it with nothing (not smoking). People trying to eliminate between-meal snacking take one behavior (eating) and replace it with nothing (not eating).

You cannot replace something with nothing. There will be times when the habitual behavior is called to mind and the goal to perform that behavior will become active. If you don't create new memories that interfere with the habit, then the old memories will continue to be retrieved. Despite your best intentions, you'll be forced to use willpower to fight off the urge to perform the behavior you are trying to change.

REPLACE SOMETHING WITH SOMETHING ELSE

Let's return to the example of trying to stop eating snacks while watching television. One possibility for trying to change this behavior would be to take up a hobby that you can do with your hands while you watch TV. You could learn a craft like crocheting or set up a jigsaw puzzle on the coffee table near the television. These activities can often be done while you watch TV, because neither activity requires intense concentration. As this new behavior becomes a habit, it will be called to mind in the situations that used to trigger the old behavior.

There are two general benefits to replacing something with something else.

First, you begin to associate a new behavior with the environment that used to call the habit to mind in the past. So, the new behavior makes the environment less strongly associated with the habit that you're trying to replace.

Second, as the new behavior becomes a habit, it will have its own goal associated with it. This new goal competes with the old goal and helps dampen the cravings that go along with stopping the old behavior. That is, adding a new habit gives your motivational system something to do, so that it doesn't get stuck on the behavior that you're trying to change.

To summarize, a key element of habit change is that you must replace old habits with new behaviors. The new behavior changes the relationship between the environment and the old habit by associating new behaviors with an environment that was associated with the old habit. The new habit also adds a new goal that will be called to mind to compete with the goal that was related to the old habit.

INSTALLING A NEW HABIT

Make no mistake, though, habit change is difficult. There are two things that often stand in the way of successful behavior change. The first is a lack of real commitment to changing the habit. The second is difficulty identifying all of the triggers for the old behavior.

Unfortunately, the punch line to the old joke holds true.

Q. How many psychologists does it take to change a lightbulb?

A. Only one, but the lightbulb has to *want* to change.

Many academic studies suggest that you will not be successful at creating lasting habit change unless you really commit to the process. Just as you are unlikely to be successful at coercing someone else to change a behavior unless that person makes a commitment to change, you will not make changes in yourself without a similar commitment.

Even after committing to habit change, it is important to identify elements of your life that support your current habits. Without knowing what triggers the behavior you want to change, you will not succeed despite your best intentions. After all, you cannot change your environment or engage your willpower effectively if you are not aware of the circumstances that drive your unwanted behaviors. To start on the road to habit change, then, you need to become mindful of the things you do mindlessly.

To this end, I recommend that you start your process of habit change with a *habit diary*. Carry a small notebook around with you. Whenever you notice that you are about to perform that habitual behavior (or that you have just done it), make a note of the date, the time of day, your mood, where you were and what you were thinking about.

While keeping the habit diary, don't spend a lot of time analyzing what you are doing. Just note your impressions of the situation.

At the end of each week, go back over the diary and start looking for patterns. Is there a particular time of day when you are performing the behavior? Are there particular settings in which it happens most? Are there particular people who seem to trigger the behavior? Are there people in your life who help keep you away from your bad habits? Are you most likely to engage in your habit when you are happy or sad or anxious?

The habit diary gives you a chance to learn about yourself, and gradually, you will come to a greater understanding of the factors that triggered the habit.

At the beginning, you may wish to avoid those situations in which you perform the undesired behavior as you change your behavior to create Smart Habits. In other trigger situations, you may want to introduce a new behavior that will gradually replace an undesired behavior. In either case, being mindful will help you engage some willpower to help get you through the initial phases.

Even after you start the process of habit change, you should continue to keep the habit diary for a while. There are a few reasons to keep going. First, keeping a diary helps you become more aware of when you are performing the behavior you are trying to change. Awareness of the behavior helps prevent you from continuing to perform it mindlessly. Second, as you progress with habit change, you may discover situations in which you are still performing the behavior. Third, you may also discover situations in which you wanted to perform the old behavior, but found ways to resist it successfully. Fourth, over time you should begin to notice that you are performing the undesired behavior less often, which will give you some positive feedback that you are successfully changing your behavior.

Most of what we have talked about so far in this chapter

focuses on *physical habits.* That is, the habits involve behaviors that you perform to act on the world. Eating, smoking, driving, and reaching for the sticky notes under your monitor are all physical habits.

Smart Thinking will ultimately require you to develop good *mental habits* as well as good physical habits. A mental habit is one that you develop to help with your thinking processes. These mental processes may also involve physical objects (like lists), but you have constructed these objects to assist with your ability to think.

Consider the organizational strategies that you may have for getting things done. Perhaps you keep a written to-do list or you carry a smartphone that keeps track of your schedule. You have probably developed habits associated with these devices. You may keep a to-do list on your desk in a particular place. You may check it at regular times during the day. You may routinely delete entries as soon as you complete them and add new ones as soon as they are assigned.

These behaviors also become habits. By keeping your to-do list in the same place all the time, you ensure a consistent mapping between the environment and a behavior.

In the chapters that follow, I'll talk about how to ensure that you have High-Quality Knowledge and that you can use that knowledge effectively. Ultimately, you want to have Smart Habits that allow you to implement the formula for Smart Thinking as a part of your daily routine.

The Takeaway

The mind is constantly looking to create habits. The main benefit of a habit is to take a process that required attention to start with and to turn it into something that can be retrieved effortlessly from memory. Because your mind is a habit-creating machine, any time there is a consistent and repeated mapping between your physical and mental world and some behavior, you have the conditions to form habits.

It is crucial to remember that most of your habits are good. They allow you to perform actions without having to think about them. As a result, you can focus your mental effort on issues of interest to you rather than on the routine aspects of your life.

To engage Smart Thinking, you want to ensure you have consistent mappings between your environment and desirable behaviors that will support Smart Habits. Make sure that you are not spending valuable time and mental energy on tasks that could and should become automatic.

While habits (good or bad) can be created unconsciously, there are three cases in which acquiring good habits requires some effort. First, you may have to organize your environment to create consistent mappings. Second, you may need to develop a practice schedule to provide enough repetitions of the behavior to generate a habit. Third, when you need to *change* an existing habit, you will have to make a conscious effort to do so.

There are two critical components of habit change. The first is to find ways to stop performing the old behavior. The mental processes that stop old behaviors are effortful and can be interfered with easily. Thus it is important to change the environment that triggers a bad habit in the first place and reduce or eliminate the stress and strenuous continual self-regulation that interfere with your ability to change.

The second crucial part of habit change is to replace the bad habit with a good one. Because habits are actions that are retrieved from memory, you cannot be successful with habit change if you try to replace something with nothing. Sheer willpower alone is not effective. Instead, replace one habit with another. The new habit interferes with the old one and gradually allows it to replace the undesired behavior.

Finally, because you carry out habits automatically, you need to become mindful of mindless behaviors to support habit change. It helps to create a habit diary to identify what triggers your habits so you can change elements of your environment to minimize the number of situations in which the habit will be engaged and so you can prepare to use your willpower when a situation that promotes the bad habit cannot be avoided.

THREE

Promoting Quality Learning by Knowing Your Limits

The mind imposes limits when perceiving and thinking about the world.

The mind may limit what you can remember about past events.

Use your awareness of these limits to improve the quality of your knowledge.

AT ANY GIVEN MOMENT, THE WORLD AROUND YOU is infinitely busy, yet you are aware of only a small amount of that activity because how you relate to and process the information—your cognitive world— is limited.

Think about going to a baseball game: There you are in the stands, sharing the game with thousands of other fans. Out on the field, there are nine fielders and several umpires moving around. The batter is at the plate waiting for a pitch. A runner takes a lead off second base. The scoreboard flashes statistics and pictures of fans in the stands. Overhead, a blimp flies around the stadium as a few light clouds float by. A fan behind you hurls an insult at a player from the visiting team. A vendor announces peanuts for sale as he walks in the aisle.

Despite all of this bustle, you are really paying attention only to a small amount of it. You might be watching only the pitcher as he prepares to throw the pitch. While you focus on the pitcher, the batter is preparing his stance for the pitch. The catcher is shifting behind him. The manager is flashing signs from the dugout. But you're not seeing any of that. You are processing only a very small fraction of what is going on in the world at any one time.

When the game is over, your memory of the entire experience contains even less information. You might remember a particular home run and that the home team won the game. Ultimately, an exciting experience has been reduced to a few images in your mind and the knowledge of the outcome.

What this example shows is that the world itself has a limitless number of events that are going on simultaneously. But your cognitive world is more narrow. A huge panoramic video camera might have captured much of the activity from the game to be played back later, but you did not. By paying attention to some things, there were others that did not make the cut.

As you transfer the information about what is happening in the world from your short-term experience to your long-term memory, the amount of available information gets even smaller. That is why only shards of the complete experience of being at the game are left for you to recall.

It is important to recognize the limitations both in what you can perceive at any given moment as well as in what you ultimately transfer to memory. Understanding these limitations and working with them is the first step to thinking smarter.

I call these limitations the *Role of 3*. When you are experiencing some event (like a baseball game), of the many things that are actually occurring in your environment, you are paying attention to about three of them at a time. For example, you might think about the pitcher, the batter, and the ball, but not the scoreboard, the crowd, the peanut vendor, or the runners on base. Later, your memory for that event is also going to be organized around roughly three of the events that you experienced during the game.

This chapter explores the way your mind limits what you process while you are participating in an event. It goes on to discuss how that information gets transferred from experience to your long-term memory and the additional limitations that are created in that transfer. Finally, the fact that you remember only a small fraction of what you encounter is used to generate recommendations about how to improve the quality of what you remember about events in the future.

What You Can Learn from Continuity Editors

In the production of a movie, a number of people take responsibility for maintaining the visual continuity of the scenes of a film. A script supervisor works with the director to try to make sure that key elements of the situation don't change from shot to shot. The film editor and a continuity editor then look carefully at the footage to identify inconsistencies from one shot to the next. Often, what you see on the movie screen is drawn from a series of takes that may have been filmed over a period of hours or even days. So, a clock in the background of a shot may read 2 p.m. in one shot and 4 p.m. in another. A glass of water might be on the left of an actor in one take and on the right in another. The continuity editor is supposed to spot these errors.

Despite all the care that Hollywood takes to eliminate these mistakes, most major films have a lot of them. In fact, there are whole websites devoted to allowing movie fans the opportunity to find the continuity errors in popular movies. Out of curiosity, I checked out James Cameron's *Avatar* at the website Movie Mistakes (www.moviemistakes.com), which provided a list of 20 continuity errors found by amateur film sleuths. One astute observer pointed out that in one scene a character is putting golf balls. In the initial shot, there are two golf balls next to each other on the ground. The scene cuts away and then back to the ground, and now the golf balls on the ground are farther apart.

What is really fascinating about these continuity errors is that most of us generally don't notice them. Despite the rich movie experience that we have while watching a big-budget motion picture, we rarely notice the many small changes from cut to cut that have crept into the movie. I know that when I first saw the movie *Avatar*, I did not notice these errors. Though after reading the list, I was able to see them when watching the movie again.

Seeing Less Than You Expect to See

Psychologists Dan Simons (coauthor of the book *The Invisible Gorilla*) and Dan Levin have studied the question of what we see and remember in complex situations. In one study, they took the idea of continuity into the real world. An experimenter dressed as a construction worker approached someone on the street to ask for directions. Halfway through the conversation, two people carrying a door walked between the research participant and the experimenter. The experimenter switched places with the person carrying the back of the door, so that suddenly the participant was talking to someone new. Few of the people in this study recognized that when the conversation continued, they were actually speaking to someone else.

This phenomenon is called *change blindness*. Even though you believe that you are seeing everything that is happening, you may fail to notice rather large changes in the environment. In a movie, objects may shift from place to place from one cut to another without anyone in the audience recognizing the changes. Even in real life, you are not always keeping track of the fine details of most of the objects around you.

Change blindness occurs because the system that processes visual information assumes the world is stable and predictable. We rightly believe that objects in the world will not suddenly change their identity. So, we accept and operate under the premise that the mind doesn't need to keep track of every detail about the objects in our environment, such as specific information about what things look like or exactly where they are located. As a result, we do not notice changes in appearance or location unless they are somehow crucial for the task we are doing at that moment. When watching *Avatar*, you are focused on the conversation between the character putting in his office and the scientist, and so the location of the golf balls on the floor is not important. If you were playing a game of golf, though, the position of the balls on the green is crucial, and then you would notice if someone moved the balls around. Change blindness is an excellent example of how little information actually has a chance to become a part of your later memories of any event.

From this example, it is clear that very little of the information in the world makes it into your head. It turns out that as you encounter a situation, there are a variety of stages in which the information is winnowed down. First, the construction of our sensory systems (like our eyes, ears, nose, and skin) that allow us to perceive the world limits what we can take in. Consider vision as an example. Humans have two eyes that face forward. As a result, the images from our two eyes overlap quite a bit. This setup has the advantage that it helps us see images in depth (because matching up the images from each eye gives us information about how far away things are in the world), but it limits our field of view. We have at most about 100 degrees of vision on each side, and so we can see about 200 degrees, meaning that we see what is in front of us and slightly to the side. Everything behind us is completely invisible.

The situation is actually more extreme than that. Each eye is set up so that you get really high-quality information only for a very small area in the middle of where the eye is looking. To get a sense of the size of this area of high-quality vision, stick your arm straight out and raise your thumb. Look at your thumb. The area of high-quality vision is about the size of your thumbnail. The rest of the visual information you get is much less clear. In fact, by the time you get far to the side, you are mostly able to detect things that are moving in your field of view without knowing what they are. That is, you see things that you might then want to fix your eyes on later, and you note their location in space.

Of all of the possible aspects of the world that you might take in visually, there is only a little bit at any moment that you are able to see with high resolution. To construct an understanding of what is outside your area of high-quality vision, your eyes are constantly in motion, scanning across the environment. From the earliest stages of vision, then, you are focused on just a small amount of the information that you could possibly take in. But, at the same time, you are building up your knowledge about what is in the environment bit by bit.

WHAT YOU SEE DEPENDS ON WHAT YOU KNOW

It is important to understand how vision works, because from the first time you start looking at a situation, you are also making use of your existing knowledge. If you are at a baseball game, how do you know where to look? If you have never been to a game before, then the whole thing is probably a complex jumble. You may miss a lot of the action, because you can't predict what is going to happen next. As you learn more about baseball and develop some expertise, you learn where to look and what objects are important to find. At first you might focus on the pitcher and hitter. Later still, you might notice whether the infield is playing in or back, or you might check out where the outfielders have chosen to stand for a particular hitter. The more you know about baseball, the more that knowledge informs how you see a game.

The baseball color commentator Tim McCarver has an uncanny ability to predict events when he is announcing a baseball game. As a former Major League catcher for the Philadelphia Phillies, he developed the Smart Habit of scanning the field to make sure that his players were in the right position for each hitter. He carried that skill to the announcing booth. Frequently, when working a game on television, he will point out that the infielders are playing too close just before a hitter lofts a looping fly ball to the shallow outfield for a single. The typical baseball fan will never notice the details that McCarver sees as a matter of routine. His knowledge of the game guides what he sees.

At any given time, what you see is a combination of the light bouncing off surfaces in the world and your existing knowledge that tells you where to look next and how to interpret what you are seeing. Psychologists call simple visual information like the colors, shapes, and sizes of objects "low-level information" and conceptual information "high-level information." I call the information that the eyes gather from the visual world itself *bottom-up seeing*, because vision is using the low-level information available from the world. I call the use of existing knowledge about the world *top-down seeing*, because vision is being guided by existing high-level knowledge

Top-down seeing plays an important role in the way we gather new information. From the moment we open our eyes, we are being guided in part by what we know already. As a result, we are most likely to acquire new information that is related to the way we think the world works. A baseball expert like McCarver notices all sorts of subtle aspects of the interactions among the players. Thus there is real value to having expertise, and that value starts having an effect on thinking from the moment that the expert starts looking at the world.

At the same time, knowledge can trap you into ways of seeing. A young girl going to her first baseball game may notice aspects of the crowd or the stadium or the players that McCarver won't see, because her top-down knowledge is not telling her exactly what to focus on. Instead, interesting bottom-up elements from the visual world may have more of an influence on what she takes in from the event.

What I have said so far is not specific to vision, though that provides an easy example. In hearing, there are also many limitations on what information we take in. There are always many different sounds in the world around us, but we pay attention to only a few of them. In our baseball scenario, if you listened to the insult being yelled by the fan behind you, you might have missed the call of the vendor in the aisle.

A classic psychological experiment on this topic asks a group of people to wear headphones. Spoken words are played through the headphones, but a different set of words is played to each ear. Participants are told to listen to the words being sent to one ear (say the left ear) and to repeat them aloud. When given these instructions, people are quite good at repeating the words that were spoken to that ear. However, they are unable to remember any of the words that they heard in the other ear, even if the same small set of words had been repeated a dozen times.

This example shows that much of the information that is available to your ears does not make it too far into your head. You are selecting only a small amount of that information to be processed enough to even know what words were being spoken.

How much of the sound information do you retain? The phenomenon of change blindness in vision suggests that you hold onto information about the visual world for hardly more than a fraction of a second. For sounds, you can remember about three seconds' worth of information in a type of memory called an *auditory loop*. This auditory loop is important for helping you remember the last few words when trying to understand a sentence. Imagine that someone said to you, "The airplane, which took off from Dallas, is scheduled to land in New York." In this sentence, the subject is "The airplane." Then, you get a clause that describes which airplane the speaker means (the one that took off from Dallas). Then the sentence gets on with telling you something new about the airplane (that it will land in New York). If you couldn't hold onto a few of the words in auditory memory, then by the time you got to the verb (is scheduled), you wouldn't be able to remember the subject of the sentence. Your ability to understand sentences that are spoken to you would fall apart.

You also learn to take advantage of the auditory loop to help you remember things. If you have a short list or a phone number to remember, you will probably repeat it to yourself as if you were hearing it in your mind's ear.

To see that this loop is only about three seconds long, try a simple study on yourself. Pretend you were going to win a prize if you could remember the words *cat, dog,* and *man* for 15 seconds. Close your eyes and see if you can do it.

Now, let's try another one. This time, try to remember the words *watermelon, hippopotamus,* and *supernatural* for 15 seconds. Close your eyes and give it a shot.

How did you do? Chances are, you remembered both sets of words. For the first set of words, you probably held the words in memory by repeating them to yourself for the 15 seconds. And very likely, you said those words fairly slowly. "Cat . . . dog . . . man." That is, you fit the words into a three-second loop and then repeated them.

When it came to the second set of words, you had to say them to yourself much more quickly. *Watermelon, hippopotamus,* and *supernatural* are long words. And *hippopotamus* is not that easy to say. To fit the words into that same three-second auditory loop, you had to repeat them in your head faster than you did the short words in the first list.

WORKING MEMORY

Another limitation on how much you can think about at any given moment comes from the concept of *working memory*, which refers to the amount of information that you can hold in your mind at once while you are thinking about something.

Working memory is not a separate place in your brain where you put knowledge that you are using while thinking. Instead, it is a reflection of the information that you can access. You have a vast warehouse of knowledge, but only a little of it is important at any given moment, and so your mind gives you access to only a fraction of what you know.

All of the examples presented so far are focused on two main points. First, despite the richness of the world around you, only a small amount of information from the world makes it into your mind for further processing and only a small amount of the vast store of knowledge that you have is available at any given time to influence what you are thinking about. Second, the process of taking in information requires a combination of bottom-up processing, which extracts the information from the world using the senses, and top-down processing, which allows your prior knowledge to influence what you perceive and remember.

How will knowing these two principles help you develop High-Quality Knowledge?

WHAT YOU KNOW DEPENDS ON WHAT YOU SEE

Perhaps the most important concept discussed so far is the idea of top-down processing. Though you may not be aware of it, what you know already has a huge impact on what you see and what you hear (and what you taste and smell, too). And there are two lessons you can draw from top-down processing.

First, you have to remember that the way you experience any-thing new, whether it is an event or a problem, will be affected by the way you have seen things in the past. So sometimes when you get stuck on a problem you are trying to solve, it may be that your previous experience with related problems has led you to describe that problem in the wrong way. You are seeing the problem inter-preted through all of your experience. The importance of the way you describe problems is a theme we take up later in the book.

Second, because you use your existing knowledge to interpret new events, the easiest new things for you to learn are those that are connected to what you have encountered in the past. Your knowl-edge is not a collection of disconnected facts. It is a web of connec-tions among pieces of information. This web is built up starting with the connection between existing knowledge and the way you sense the world.

To get a better idea of how your knowledge is interconnected, try a simple exercise: For the next minute make a list of all of the vegetables you can think of.

How did you do? Do you think you were able to list every vegetable you know? Most probably not.

How did you go about doing this exercise? Think for a moment about the process you went through to come up with the items on your list.

If you're like most people, you started out by listing a few things you know to be vegetables. It is interesting that you prob-ably couldn't list more than three or four vegetables that way.

Why is that? When psychologists talk about getting things out of memory, they talk about *retrieving* information. When you try to retrieve information (like the names of vegetables), the various things you know that are related to what you want to pull out of memory compete with each other. Think of the various vegetables you know as if they were a group of five-year-olds who want to be picked for a prize. Each of them jumps up high and, at the same time, tries to push down the others. The first one picked is the one that has jumped highest and pushed down on the others the hardest. Then the rest of the vegetables compete to be chosen next. After you have remembered roughly three vegetables that way, the successful items have beaten down the unsuccessful ones. You now have the mental equivalent of a group of five-year-olds lying on the floor sniffling after having been pushed to the ground. These items are hard to retrieve, and so you get stuck.

After remembering approximately three things in this way, you probably shifted to a different strategy. When I use an example like this in my classes, many people report thinking about a specific situation in which they encounter a lot of vegetables and then listing the ones that are related to that situation. You might have envisioned walking down the aisle of a grocery store, or thought about making a salad, or imagined working in your garden. As you made this mental tour, you would name all of the vegetables you saw.

Strange as it may seem, this exercise tells you something important about your memory.

Think first about how you might get a computer memory to list all of the vegetables it knows. You would probably create some kind of file that listed all of the vegetables. When you wanted to know all of the vegetables in the computer's memory, you would open this file and list the contents. I tried this by going to Google and typing "list of vegetables" in the search box. The first entry I got back was a link to an alphabetical list of vegetables. That web page had a lot more vegetables on it than I would be able to list if I did this exercise.

But human memory doesn't work like a programmed computer. Instead, memory is organized around relationships and associations. Your memory is designed to provide you with the information you are likely to need in situations in which you are likely to need it. When you enter a grocery store, your mind wants to be helpful, so it makes it easy to think about vegetables. The availability of your knowledge about vegetables helps you predict what you are going to see in the store and it calls to mind knowledge that will enable you to make decisions about what to buy. Things that you are not likely to see in the grocery store will be hard to think about. You are unlikely to see a surgeon in scrubs walking through the aisles of the store, and so your memory makes the concept of a surgeon harder to think about in the store.

More generally, any situation in which you encounter vegetables is one in which your memory will help you out by making it easier to think about them. So thinking about making a salad helps you think about the vegetables you normally put in a salad. Thinking about your refrigerator helps you think about the vegetables you find in your refrigerator. Thinking about your garden helps you to think about the vegetables you grow.

Memory is all about connections. Psychologists have demonstrated these connections using the concept of *priming*. One experimental procedure that is often used asks people to identify whether a sequence of letters forms a word by pressing one button if it is a word and a second button if it is not. If you saw the sequence *BRAKE*, you would press the button to say that the letters form a word. If you saw the letters *BRAIK*, you would press the button to say that the letters do not form a word.

After a little practice, it takes you just a fraction of a second to respond correctly whether a sequence of letters forms a word. At this point, experiments vary what is presented before you make a judgment. For example, you could just see a nonsense string of letters like *XXXXXX*, followed by the sequence *BRAKE*. The amount of time it takes you to respond that this is a word is used as a baseline for comparison. Another possibility is that you could see words that occur in similar circumstances. So you might see *CAR* and then *BRAKE*. In this case, you are faster to respond that *BRAKE* is a word than you were in the baseline test. A third possibility is that you might see an unrelated word. In this case, you might be presented with *CARROT* and then *BRAKE*. Now, you are slower to respond that *BRAKE* is a word than you were in the baseline.

Having High-Quality Knowledge, then, is not just about learning things in isolation, it is about learning the connections among things. Because you use your knowledge to help you understand new situations, you want to have good connections that enable you to bring important information to mind when you are likely to need it.

Ultimately, your memory wants to provide you with the information *you are most likely to need* when doing something. As a result, only a small portion of the huge volume of knowledge you have is available to you at any moment. The information that is most likely to be in your working memory when you are doing something is the knowledge that is somehow connected to your previous experiences that relate to that activity. Then when you learn new things, you try to connect the new information to whatever is in your working memory.

instantly smarter
Remembering Names

Do you have trouble remembering people's names when you are first introduced to them? Most people say that they do. They go to parties and are introduced to a new person, and almost immediately they realize that they cannot remember that person's name.

The discussion about the structure of memory also helps make clear why it is often difficult to remember the name of someone to whom you have just been introduced. It also suggests a few things you can do to become better at remembering names.

There are three things that make names hard to remember. First, names are arbitrary facts about people. You (probably) got your name because your parents decided to call you by that name when you were born. Most of us are not lucky enough to be able to pick our own names. Memory is best when we are able to relate new facts to what we already know, but the relationship between the name and a person is tenuous at best.

Second, information is best remembered when you use that knowledge often. We'll talk more about that in Chapter 6. But when you meet people for the first time, they are probably standing right there in front of you. You won't actually need their name until they have walked away, and so you're unlikely to use it.

Third, we often don't pay much attention to the person's name when they introduce themselves. I sometimes call this the "*Peanuts* effect" after the old cartoons on TV. In those cartoons, whenever an adult spoke, it came out as a muted trumpet going "*wa-wa-wa wa-wa-wa*." I often feel that when someone introduces himself or herself to me, the next few words after "Hi, my name is" come out as "*wa-wa-wa wa-wa-wa*."

You can use the suggestions in this box to help you remember names better and keep these key points in mind:

• When you are being introduced to someone, *pay attention*.
• Try to turn his name into something that is related to the person.

Find some aspect of the person—his eyes or hair or smile—try to relate his name to it. You will do a better job of remembering the name if you can relate it to something about the person.

• Use the person's name in conversation as quickly as possible after hearing it. Try to work it into the conversation a couple of times. It will feel a little awkward to do that, because she is standing right there, but if you do, you'll be amazed at how much better you become at remembering the names of new people.

• Remember that everyone has trouble remembering other people's names. So when you are talking to someone whose name you've forgotten, just apologize and ask him to repeat his name. Chances are he will be flattered that you cared enough to ask again. He is also likely to be relieved, because he has probably forgotten your name as well.

Working Within Your Limits

Every year in November, I go to the annual meeting of the Psychonomic Society. The word *psychonomic* was made up to reflect that there were psychologists who were seeking the fundamental "laws" of thought. (The Greek root *nomos* means "law.") This society was formed in the late 1950s to provide a place for scientists studying the mind to share information about their research. While the meeting is a great place to find out about cutting-edge work, there is a problem at this conference.

Lots of scientists want the chance to talk about their projects, and hundreds of talks are presented at this two-and-a-half-day meeting. To fit everything in, each talk is only about 15 minutes long. Now, think about it. If you had one chance to talk to your colleagues from around the world each year, and you only had

15 minutes, you might be tempted to throw in as much information as you can in that brief period. And that is what happens. The talks at this conference are dense. People try to present a lot of information in a short period of time.

This conference is full of people who focus their lives on the way that humans process information and learn new facts. And yet, all of this knowledge about how people learn seems to get thrown out the window as soon as they have the chance to talk to their colleagues about their work. Giving very little background information, they launch into a rapid-fire discussion of experiments and data. And as a result, I often have a lot of trouble remembering *anything* from the talks I hear at the conference. Over the years, I have adopted the strategy of standing in the hallways outside the talks and stopping my colleagues to find out what they are working on. I find that these conversations give me a lot more insight into people's work than the formal talks themselves.

What is going on here?

Generally speaking, your memory for things that happened to you in the past is governed by the Role of 3. You are able to remember approximately three distinct things about any experience, whether that experience is a baseball game, a movie, or a poorly constructed conference talk. The quality of what you can remember depends on how well you are able to connect those three things to knowledge you have already. You create High-Quality Knowledge when you relate new information to important knowledge you already possess.

The Role of 3 in Action

Think back to the example of the baseball game that I used to open the chapter. Weeks or months after attending that game, you will remember approximately three facts about it. You will also remember anything that you are able to associate with those facts. For example, the first fact might be that one player hit a home run. That fact is likely to be related to the number of runners on base when the home run was hit, because that determines how many runs scored. It may also be connected to the pitcher who gave up the home run. So, remembering that there was a home run allows you to recall the other information that was related to that event.

Likewise, you might remember the final score, which might come along with associated information about the winning and losing pitchers and how the outcome of the game affected the standings. Finally, the third distinct fact might be that you ate a pretzel, which may be connected to how good hot pretzels taste at the ballpark as well as a memory of the mustard stain you ended up getting on your favorite shirt.

The key to the total amount you are ultimately able to recall lies in the interconnections among the knowledge you have. Although you may remember approximately three distinct and independent pieces of information about an event, you can call to mind quite a lot of knowledge if you have many interconnections and associations among the facts. When you tried to list vegetables, you could come up with only about three of them if you just listed words associated with the word *vegetable*. But you might have listed ten or more if you took a mental walk through your local supermarket or traversed your mental garden.

PUTTING THE ROLE OF 3 INTO PRACTICE

You can use your knowledge of the Role of 3 to influence what you remember about events and to use it to affect what other people remember about their encounters with you. Following the guidelines I present is both straightforward to carry out and difficult to do without discipline. After all, even many of my colleagues at the Psychonomic Society Conference end up presenting information in a way that makes it hard for me to remember anything later. To develop High-Quality Knowledge from this meeting, I had to find another way to learn about my colleagues' research. Ultimately, the talks given by my colleagues would be more effective if they respected the Role of 3.

Acquiring High-Quality Knowledge means learning to get the most out of presentations, meetings, and other encounters where you are expected to pick up new information. By knowing the Role of 3 and respecting it, you can improve the way you learn.

If you look carefully at your own behavior, you may discover that you frequently leave your memory for events, classes, lectures, and meetings up to chance. That is, you are probably not very strategic about trying to control what you remember. Now, if the event in question is a baseball game, it probably doesn't matter what you remember about it later. Any memory is likely to be a pleasant one. You had no particular goal in mind when you decided to go to the game, so it doesn't really matter what you recall about it in the future.

But suppose you have just attended an hour-long business

meeting. A number of issues were discussed, a plan for future projects was laid out, and representatives of different work groups gave input on ongoing projects. Lots of other things happened at the meeting as well. Someone told a really funny joke. There was a rumor about possible layoffs in the future. As always the meeting ran a little late. The meeting has just ended, and you have to hurry off to your next appointment.

Ideally, you would remember the most important content of that meeting. You would be focused on the plans for future products and updates on work group meetings. It would be a shame if your memory for these important elements of the meeting were crowded out by the great joke or the anxiety-provoking rumors of pending layoffs.

If you are like most people, though, you don't spend any time trying to influence what you remember later. Instead, you gather your things together after a meeting, and walk off focusing your thoughts on the next event on your schedule. These days, the end of a meeting is greeted by the emergence of smartphones as people check to see what emails and texts they may have missed in the last hour. People who are running really late might even call ahead to the next meeting to apologize.

By walking off so quickly, though, you are not exerting any control over your own memory.

Smart Thinking is the ability to acquire High-Quality Knowledge and Applying Knowledge when you need it. If you do not exert any control over the information you remember about events, then you are not doing your part to generate High-Quality Knowledge. Instead, you should use the Role of 3 before, during, and after important events such as meetings and classes to be proactive in controlling what you remember about situations.

Here are three simple steps to improve the quality of your memory for new events:

1. **Prepare.** Start by doing a little preparation for any class, meeting, or presentation. Since you will most likely have at least a general idea of the content to be discussed in any given situation, you can prepare by thinking about what you are hoping to get out of it. You are most likely to be able to remember information that you connect to what you know already; thus this mental preparation helps ensure your existing knowledge will be available in your working memory. As a result, when topics relating to what you hope to learn are raised, you will be prepared to connect them to your existing knowledge. Educational psychologists call this list of topics an *advance organizer*.

   If you are attending a meeting, talk, or event for which no information or agenda has been provided to you in advance, you should spend a little time thinking about what is most likely to be discussed. Prepare yourself by thinking about the issues you hope are raised and think about how that information might relate to other projects or ideas you are working on.

   At other times, you will get some advance information about what is to come. Make sure that you actually use any advance organizers that are provided to you. Years ago, I wrote a textbook for classes in cognitive psychology with two colleagues, Doug Medin and Brian Ross. Each chapter started with an outline that highlighted the topics that were going to be covered. The aim was to provide an *advance organizer* for students to use to prepare themselves for the topics that would be covered in the chapter. I always suspected that students skipped the outline. Eventually, I started talking about the

value of advance organizers and asked how many students
ignored the outline. The laughter that greeted this question was
my signal that they generally skipped over the outline, and so
they didn't benefit from the chance to activate a little of their
knowledge before diving into the chapter.

2. **Pay attention.** Thinking is hard work. If you do not keep your
working memory clear, then you are undermining your ability
to think about what is going on in your class or meeting.

This might seem obvious, but if you look around the room
at many meetings, you will find yourself face-to-face with
one of the true demons of modern life: *multitasking*. Sitting in a
meeting, you will see that some people are taking care of work
that is unrelated to the current meeting. Others are checking
their email on their smartphones. Still others are reading. Each
of these activities sucks up your working memory. You cannot
maximize the quality of the new knowledge you are taking in
if you do not give yourself every opportunity to pay attention.

The dangers of multitasking are finally starting to get some
attention in the media, but psychologists have known about
them for a long time. For decades, research has explored *dual
task performance*. That is, studies have examined how people's
performance breaks down when you try to do two or more
things at once.

The lesson from this research is that when people are
doing complex thinking, they don't really divide their attention
evenly across the things they have to do. Instead, they *time
share*. They do a little of one task and then a little of another.
And they flip back and forth between the tasks. And sometimes that is fine. For example, after you have been driving for
a few years, keeping your car on the road does not require a lot

of effort. If you are cruising on the highway, you can check out the cars in front of you every second or so and make some general decisions about whether you want to change lanes. Because you don't need to exert a lot of mental effort to drive, you can also have a conversation or listen to the radio.

But what if it starts raining and there is an accident up ahead on the road? Now the task of driving requires more effort. If you continue trying to have a conversation or listening to the radio, then your driving performance will suffer. In the car, you have some control over the situation, so you may find that you stop talking and shut the radio off to deal with the change in conditions.

Meetings are the same way. If the meeting is important, and there are issues that need to be addressed and remembered, then whenever you try to do something else (like check your email or do other work), you are pulling your attention away from the meeting.

The research on multitasking goes a bit further, though. On average, people think that they are better-than-average multitaskers. That is, everyone is willing to acknowledge that some people may be hurt by trying to do a few things at once, but few people are willing to say that their own performance will really suffer significantly from multitasking.

Unfortunately, you are simply not the best judge of your own behavior, because multitasking also interferes with your ability to judge how good you are at multitasking. When you do a few things at once, it is hard to gauge how effectively you are performing any of the tasks.

So pay attention. Don't multitask.

3. **Review.** In the few minutes after a class or meeting—or even after reading a book or article—take a few seconds or minutes to write down the main points. If you are walking to another meeting and can't write, then rehearse them in your head. You might even invest in a digital recorder and say them out loud to yourself as you walk. There is evidence that saying things out loud helps you remember them later.

   Even if you never read what you write or listen to what you record, the act of producing a written or spoken summary helps you remember the information better later. One reason to buy a little digital recorder is that you may feel silly or self-conscious walking out of a meeting and talking to yourself, so the digital recorder provides you with an excuse to talk.

As you review this information, think about ways to attach what you have learned to other knowledge. These three strategies will guarantee that you develop High-Quality Knowledge.

HELP OTHERS USE THE ROLE OF 3

There are many kinds of interactions that you have with other people in which you want to affect what they remember later. These interactions range all the way from job interviews, in which you are trying to get people to remember things about you, to running a meeting or teaching a class, in which you want people to remember what the meeting or class was about.

Unfortunately, not everyone you encounter will know the Role of 3. So, it is up to you to help make everyone around you more effective by promoting a Culture of Smart. The Role of 3 suggests two general principles to keep in mind when designing presentations, classes, and other interactions with people.

- Connect new things you want people to remember to their existing knowledge.
- People will remember roughly three things about their interaction with you.

So be sure to stay focused.

To parallel the three recommendations I made for maximizing the High-Quality Knowledge you obtain from others, here are three suggestions for improving *what people remember about you*.

1. **Start all of your presentations with an advance organizer.**
   Just as you want to form an idea of what is going to happen in a meeting or talk you attend, you want to provide information to others to give them a sense of what is to come. This advance organizer does not need to be detailed. A sentence about each of the main topics is enough to get everyone thinking.

   One purpose of the advance organizer is to get people prepared to use some of their existing knowledge. It is crucial that people attach new knowledge to things they already know. Giving people information about what will be coming in your presentation gives them the opportunity to activate the knowledge they already have in preparation for learning. In the interests of time, my colleagues often dive into their talks without preparing the audience. So, it takes awhile for people listening to the talk to figure out how to connect the content to things they already know.

   The advance organizer also focuses your presentation on a

small number of items. A common mistake in preparing presentations is to try to provide too much information. If you find that your advance organizer runs much longer than three items, that is a clear sign you are trying to present more information than people can reasonably be expected to take away. Cut yourself back to about three items. You will quickly find that your presentations are much more effective and people remember more about them.

If you can't limit yourself back to a small number of items, then try to find some relationships among the items on your agenda. If you can find ways that the items interrelate, then perhaps you can turn what seems like a large number of disconnected pieces into a smaller number of connected groups of information.

2. **During a presentation, stay focused primarily on your three main points.** The more digressions and other interesting facts you add, the more likely it is that people will remember something other than the essential message you are hoping to convey.

You may be afraid that by focusing on only your main points you won't be saying enough. It may feel as if you were repeating yourself if you keep a meeting or class focused on only three items. Remember, though, that when you give people new information, they do not know it as well as you. This repetition provides people with an opportunity to focus on the key information and to elaborate on it while learning.

To help people learn new information, find ways to help them connect this content to their existing knowledge. Whole books have been written on giving effective presentations, so I am not going to go on about this point at length. One specific suggestion I have, however, is to encourage people to think of ways in which they would be able to use the information you are presenting. Then, when they encounter those usage situations later, they will be more likely to remember what you told them.

Of course, one may argue that the world has simply gotten too busy to focus on only three items. It is hard to get people together for meetings, and so it is vital to go through as many items as possible when you have everyone in the same room. This comment is a variation of the motivation my colleagues in the Psychonomic Society have to present a huge amount of information in a 15-minute talk. The Role of 3 is to be respected, not circumvented. It applies regardless of how busy you are and how much information you would ideally like to present. Beefing up the agenda for a meeting is going to succeed only at having each person remember a different set of facts from the meeting. And that is not going to create a Culture of Smart.

3. **At the end of every presentation, summarize your three key points.** This summary ensures that you have the chance to emphasize the elements you believe were most important for people to know. In addition, even if other people do not take the time to review what they have learned, this summary gives them one additional chance to rehearse the new information.

   I find this summary to be particularly important at the end of individual meetings that I have with people. As a professor, I meet regularly with graduate students. Over the course of an hour, we may have a free-ranging conversation that does not have the structure of a lecture or group meeting. As a result, it is helpful to end the meeting with a list of the action items. That review ensures that my student and I agree on what has to happen to follow up on the issues we discussed.

In an effort to practice what I preach, the chapters of this book have been organized using the principles I have suggested. As you have probably noted, each chapter begins with three sentences that let you know what is coming. Reading the advance organizer will get you thinking about what is to come in the chapter. I have also tried to keep my digressions to a minimum. In fact, one reason for the Instantly Smarter boxes is to mark certain ideas that might be slightly off topic but are relevant to your quest to become a Smart Thinker. These boxes can be read separately and thought about independently from the other material in the chapters. Each chapter ends with a set of takeaway messages that summarizes the key information from the chapter and ties it all together.

instantly smarter
Tips for Paying Attention

When you are in a meeting or class or reading a book or article, you sometimes find you are having trouble paying attention. There are a few sources of this difficulty.

The state of your body affects the state of your mind. If you are tired, then you will have trouble sustaining attention. Coffee and other caffeinated drinks can help that a little, but while caffeine will make you feel more alert, it does not seem to affect the areas of your brain that help you remember new information. So in the long run you are better off trying to add some more sleep into your schedule than you are drinking an extra cup of coffee.

If you are seated for a long period of time, you may also find that your mind wanders. In that case, stand up and stretch. Walk to the back of a meeting room or classroom and stand or pace for a minute. The activity will help you pay attention. In creating a Culture of Smart, encourage other people to stand up and move around during meetings as well. The norm in meetings is for everyone to stay seated, but that may not be ideal for learning.

Get to know your own body's rhythms. When I was in college, I used to get very tired right after eating. Eventually, I stopped taking classes in the hour right after lunch to avoid falling asleep in class. If you can't avoid a time of day that you know is bad for you, then try to take a good walk before having to sit in a class or meeting.

In addition, try to engage your entire body in the class, meeting, or book. Take notes. Even doodling on a sheet of paper has been shown to help people become more engaged in a class or meeting.

Finally, if none of the suggestions I make here works for you and you find that you are extremely distracted by noises and other things in your work environment, you might want to look up the symptoms of attention deficit disorders on the Internet. From there, you can decide whether you are a good candidate for testing. Chances are, you are not suffering from an attention deficit disorder, but when all else fails it is a possibility you should consider.

The Takeaway

The world is a busy place. There is a lot going on around you. To bring order to this chaos, the mind places limits on the information that is used at every stage. When perceiving an event, only a limited amount of the potential information in the world becomes the focus of attention. The perception of an event is a combination of bottom-up processing using information from the world and top-down processing that uses existing knowledge to constrain how we interpret new events.

During the course of an event, you have a limited capacity in your working memory. Only a small amount of what you know is available to the thought processes you are using to reason and solve new problems. One way that you increase the amount of information you consider as you think is to ensure that bits of knowledge are densely interconnected. Thus, when learning, it is important to find ways to connect new information to existing knowledge.

When you remember an event, you are likely to be able to recall about three independent bits of information about it: That is the Role of 3. It is important to use this knowledge about your memory to organize both what you remember about the events you experience and how you structure presentations to other people.

When you enter a meeting, think about what you want to get out of it. Then, pay attention to that information. At the end of any experience, spend some time repeating to yourself the key take-away messages. That way, you are exerting some control over what you remember about the situation later.

When you run a meeting or class, or you attend an interview, introduce the key points you want people to remember later. Then focus your presentation ruthlessly on those points and avoid as many digressions as you can. Finally, summarize the key points at the end so people will walk away from their interactions with you remembering what you hoped they would remember.

By bearing the Role of 3 in mind, you can help maximize the quality of your knowledge. In this way, you have a real head start on thinking smarter. In addition, by using the Role of 3 to organize presentations, you have taken a step toward creating a Culture of Smart.

FOUR

Understanding How Things Work

Causal knowledge is the information
you know about how the world works.

The quality of our causal knowledge
is less good than we think it is.

We can improve the quality of our causal
knowledge through self-explanation.

JOHANNES KEPLER GETS A BUM RAP FROM HISTORY.
Kepler was an astronomer in the late 1500s and early
1600s who is best known in modern science for his equations for
the movements of planets. At that time, people thought that the
planets moved in perfect circular orbits around the sun. Looking
at measurements by astronomers like Tycho Brahe, Kepler found
that a circular orbit did not correctly predict where the planets
were seen in the night sky. He determined that the planets move
in an elliptical orbit, and he laid out the equations that describe
those movements.

Most people who have heard about Kepler at all know him for
this achievement. As important as his equations were, though, he

also laid the groundwork for Newton's theory of the movements of the planets, which revolutionized the study of physics.

Kepler was not just interested in the paths that the planets take around the sun, he wanted to know what caused them to move. He was constantly asking, Why?

One thing he noticed was that the planets far away from the sun move more slowly than the planets close to the sun. He also knew that the light of the sun gets weaker as you get farther from the sun so that the planets farther from the sun get less light than the planets closer to the sun. He reasoned that there might be some other force coming from the sun that pushed the planets around and that less of that force reached the outer planets than the inner planets, and that is why they move more slowly.

In some of his writing, he speculated about an animating force that would move outward from the sun (like light does) that somehow pushed the planets around in their orbits. He struggled to make this idea work. Unfortunately, he could not find a way to change a force moving outward from the sun into movement around the sun. To try to solve this problem, Kepler brought in knowledge from other areas. Because Kepler was also aware of the scientific interest in magnets and magnetism at the time, he toyed with the idea that the sun is like a magnet that pulls the planets inward. Again, though, he had trouble finding a way to get a force pulling inward to account for an orbit that goes around the sun. After all, a movement inward ought to bring the planets crashing into the sun.

Kepler was oh so close to the correct reason the planets orbit the sun. A magnet attracts iron toward it. The sun's gravitational force attracts the planets toward it as well. What Kepler was missing was a mechanism that would allow the planets to move given a force pulling inward. About 80 years later, Isaac Newton produced his laws of motion and answered the question. Newton was the one who figured out that forces change the motion of objects and are not required to keep objects in motion. Of course, Newton is now the big name in history. Kepler's fame, if we can call it that, is just for the equations for the orbits of the planets. History rewards the people who succeed.

The Big Question: Why?

A key aspect of Kepler's Smart Thinking was his interest in the question *why*. It turns out that to one degree or another, everyone wants to know why the world works as it does. However, engaging in Smart Thinking requires exceptionally good answers to that question.

Getting answers to *why* questions plays a key role in everyday life: You walk into your living room and flip on the light switch. The switch is supposed to control a lamp that sits on a table by the sofa, but when you turn on the switch, nothing happens. There is some light coming in through the window, so it isn't completely dark. You walk over to the lamp and jiggle it a bit, but still the room stays dark. You check the electrical cord that emerges from behind the lamp and follow it to the outlet, but it is plugged in. You flip the switch on the base of the lamp, but it is on. Finally, you unscrew the lightbulb and shake it. You hear that familiar rattling sound, so you walk to the closet and replace the bulb with one of those new energy-efficient fluorescent bulbs. You turn the switch on the wall back on, and the light flickers to life.

That was Smart Thinking.

When you go through a simple troubleshooting exercise like this one, even with devices at home, you are doing some pretty sophisticated reasoning. You are using your knowledge about why things work to help you solve a problem. You know that flipping the light switch causes electricity to be available at an electrical outlet, and so you check to see whether the lamp is plugged in. You know that sometimes your particular lamp has a loose connection in it, and so jiggling it may cause it to come on. You know that there is a switch on the lamp that may accidentally get shut off. Finally, when all else fails, the bulb in the lamp may have blown out. You know that when the bulb blows, there is a filament in it that no longer creates an electrical connection. Pieces of the filament are often broken and so they will rattle around the inside of the bulb if you shake it. This exercise involved testing each of the explanations for why the lamp might not be working.

The ability to think about why things work and what may be causing problems when events do not go as expected seems like an obvious aspect of the way we think. It is interesting that this ability to think about why things happen (and what has gone wrong with them) is one of the key abilities that separates human abilities from those of just about every other animal on the planet.

Asking *why* allows people to create explanations. Isaac Newton didn't just see an apple fall from a tree. He used that observation to help him figure out why it fell. Your car mechanic doesn't just observe that your car is not working, he figures out why it is not working using knowledge about why it usually does work properly. Your doctor doesn't just look at your symptoms, she reasons about why you are sick so she can treat you. And anyone who has spent time with a five-year-old knows that children this age can test the limits of your patience by trying to get explanations for why everything works as it does.

Psychologists call the ability to generate explanations for things *causal reasoning*. Why does an understanding of causes matter?

Let's take an example of the difference between the way humans use tools and the way that our close cousins chimpanzees use tools. According to psychologist Daniel Povinelli, one of the big differences between apes (like chimps) and humans is that humans naturally reason about why things work and chimps do not. That is, humans are very good at causal reasoning, and chimps are not.

Tool use doesn't separate chimps from humans, because chimps also use tools. In the wild, there are chimp communities that use rocks to smash nuts and others that use thin reeds to fish for termites in mounds. In laboratory situations, chimps can learn to use tools, as well, but they do not seem to learn why the tools work.

Take an example from Povinelli's research. He puts a piece of food in the center of a clear tube that is too small for the chimp to reach in. The chimp can see the food and wants to get it. There are sticks nearby, and eventually, the chimp learns to insert the stick into the tube to push the food out. A human doing this task realizes that the stick pushes the food along the tube in the direction away from where the stick was inserted.

Chimps don't seem to get this. After the chimp learns to get the food out using the stick, Povinelli puts a trap at the bottom of the tube on one side so that the food will fall into the trap if it is pushed over it. Initially, chimps will select the side that they insert the stick haphazardly, not realizing that pushing the food in one direction will cause it to land in the trap rather than coming out. After a while, the chimps learn to insert the stick into the side closest to the trap so that the food is pushed out the other end.

Even at this point, chimps don't appear to understand what they are doing, though. Once a chimp learns to deal with this trap, Povinelli starts putting the food on the other side of the trap rather than in the middle of the tube. Now, if the chimp continues to put the stick in the side closest to the trap, the food will get pushed into the trap. And that is what happens. The chimp doesn't understand that the stick is pushing the food through the tube.

This game continues. The chimps will eventually learn to deal with this situation as well, and when they do, Povinelli changes it again so that a chimp who really understood the way the tool worked would respond correctly, but one who just learned a particular strategy would not. Each time, the chimps fail until they get a lot of experience using the tool in a different way.

This line of studies suggests that chimps are not doing causal reasoning. They are not able to figure out why things work the way they do. They search around seemingly at random for actions that are effective. Then they learn a relationship between a situation, an action, and an outcome. If they find an action that works, they keep trying it in the future. So they learn *that* one particular action is effective, but not *why* it is effective. Without knowing why, the chimp cannot cope when the situation changes in subtle ways that make the action ineffective.

From an early age, humans act differently. Like chimps, people learn about how their actions affect the world. Unlike chimps, though, people also seek to understand why. As a result, when a tool we have been using does not work, we prefer not to proceed by trial-and-error until we find a way to make it work. Instead, we want to figure out the reason why the tool no longer works and then fix the problem.

Of course, there are times when you have no causal understanding of something and there is no clear way to understand it in that context. You might try trial-and-error processing in that situation. For example, I remember watching my grandfather deal with the television in his living room. Sometimes, the picture would get fuzzy. He would first play with the antenna on top of the TV. If that didn't work, he'd check the connection between the antenna and the back of the television. When all else failed, he'd give a sharp whack to the side of the TV. He didn't seem to have any clear causal understanding of how the TV worked, but in the past one of those actions would often fix the problem. Because it was hard to understand how the TV worked, and there were not a lot of good resources for learning about TVs, he could not engage in much Smart Thinking to fix the picture on the screen.

Psychologist Michael Tomasello argues that this ability to think about why things happen is a crucial reason humans have complex cultures and chimps do not. Imagine that you are watching someone use a new tool. You don't just focus on the movements she is making and the outcomes of those movements. You are also interested in a variety of causal aspects of the situation. You want to understand the goal that someone is trying to achieve by using the tool. You want to understand something about how the tool works. You may not understand all of the details, but you do try to get some sense of why the tool succeeds in achieving the goal.

Think about the first time you saw someone in your house using a vacuum cleaner. Perhaps your mom was cleaning the living room. It must have seemed strange to you as a child that your mother was pushing a large and loud object back and forth across the floor. If you could not understand what she was doing, then you probably asked her why she was engaged in such a strange and loud behavior, and she explained that she was trying to clean the floor. After that, you probably asked why the loud machine was able to clean the floor, and she probably gave you an explanation that involved dirt being sucked into the machine. You probably didn't understand the fine details of how vacuums work at that point (or even why someone would bother cleaning if the room was only going to get dirty again), but part of learning about vacuums involved some amount of causal knowledge.

Because people want to know both why others do what they do as well as why the tools people use are effective, they can also begin to contemplate ways to improve those tools. Sticking with the vacuum for a moment, people have always wanted to clean their surroundings. The concept of cleanliness appears in ancient texts. Archaeologists have discovered ancient forms of brooms and mops. The vacuum is just another way of trying to achieve the same goal of cleaning using a more sophisticated device. It would occur to someone to try to develop a vacuum only if they understood that people want to find ways to clean and also that a combination of suction and a filter would provide a way to clean a surface.

Similarly, James Dyson was able to invent the cyclone vacuum in part because he realized that once you had a vacuum cleaner, the difficult problem to be solved was separating the dirt from the air sucked into it.

Because people are interested in causality, they often find products appealing when the products give some indication of how they work. In an old-style vacuum, the bag would inflate as soon as the machine was switched on, and you could hear particles being sucked into it. The Dyson vacuum uses clear plastic to give people a sense that they can watch it in action. Other kinds of products do this as well. For example, pills with two kinds of medicine in them will often use different colors for each side of the pill to highlight that there are two active ingredients. Capsules with different kinds of medicine in them often have little balls of different colors to signal the many active ingredients.

Overall, our ability to ask and answer the question *why* leads us to build on the innovations of past generations to create new more sophisticated tools. Tomasello refers to this process as *ratcheting up the complexity of cultures*. In a culture in which people ask why, each generation can begin with the current set of tools in use as a baseline and try to improve those tools from that starting point.

Let's return to chimps: In the wild, chimps do have cultures of a sort. If one chimp accidentally learns that banging a rock on a nut breaks it open, eventually the other chimps in the group will also learn to bang rocks and break nuts. They learn this by imitating the actions of the other chimp. They will bang rocks when they are around nuts. Eventually, one of the nuts breaks, and the chimp has learned that banging a rock can help to break a nut.

Chimps don't teach each other, though. To be able to teach, you have to know that someone else has the goal to learn. And to learn from someone else, you have to think about what they are trying to achieve. Chimps don't really explain to themselves why other chimps are acting like they do, and so they do not have an understanding of what it would mean to teach.

Also, chimp tool cultures don't get any more complex. None of the chimps tries to find a better way to do what he is doing. It doesn't even occur to them to try because they are not thinking about why their tools work in the first place.

The ability to think about why things work is a huge part of what makes humans smart. The more causal understanding you have, the higher the quality of your knowledge overall. And High-Quality Knowledge is central to the formula for Smart Thinking.

The Organization of Causal Knowledge

To understand the power of causal knowledge, it is important to be aware of how your causal knowledge is organized and how it is used to solve new problems.

Your causal knowledge is organized around explanations. That is, causal knowledge is always related to a particular *why* question. There are two important aspects of causal knowledge that result from the relationship between causes and explanations.

The first key aspect of causal knowledge is that there are often many different explanations for the same event. These explanations typically account for a variety of different factors that may affect a situation. Some of these factors may be physical, whereas others may be social or even psychological.

A car company might issue a recall for one million cars that have faulty accelerator pedals. Why did the company issue this recall? The answers to this question explain the variety of factors that led to the recall. Some of the explanations might be physical (a worn part inside the accelerator caused it to stick sometimes). Some explanations might be related to the sociology of business (a desire to increase market share quickly led to a decrease in quality control and oversight of manufacturers of parts). Still other explanations might relate to consumer psychology (initiating a recall might boost public perception that the company cares about safety).

Each of these explanations can be evaluated against the facts in the case. The first explanation for why the accelerator sticks might be that there is a worn part in it. However, this explanation can be tested, perhaps by taking apart some of the broken accelerators. These tests might reveal that the initial explanation was mistaken and that the accelerator sticks because of a faulty spring inside it.

For any event, though, there are a number of different explanations that can all be correct simultaneously. Each of these explanations addresses a different component of an event. So, each type of causal information is relevant to helping answer different kinds of questions. Someone learning to design a new accelerator might learn from the physical mistakes made in the device. Another person learning about how businesses should handle recalls might learn from the consumer psychology explanation.

The second important aspect of our causal knowledge is that it is *nested*. That is, whenever you give an explanation, it is always possible to ask *why* again and to give an explanation at a more specific level. Five-year-olds learn this trick quickly, and they will continue to press adults for more and more specific explanations of an event.

To return to the car example, a general explanation for the recall might be that the accelerator on the car sticks, leading it to get into accidents. Asking why the car accelerator sticks leads to a deeper explanation that one part inside the accelerator wears down and catches against a second part. Asking why this part wears down leads to yet another and even deeper explanation that the plastic used to make the part expands when heated, causing it to rub against the casing it is contained in. Asking why the part expands leads to an even deeper explanation about the molecular behavior of that type of plastic when it heats.

The key here is that each explanation addresses a particular question. Once you build that explanation, though, it is always possible to ask another more specific question. Answering that question involves generating another more specific explanation. And so on. That process never ends.

CAUSAL KNOWLEDGE AND EXPERT PROBLEM SOLVING

The reason we care about causal knowledge is because it is crucial for solving new problems.

Chapter 2 explored Smart Habits. Habits are the things you do to solve problems that are so familiar that you don't need to think about them. That is, if you already know the answer to a question, you rely on your memory for the solution and do the same thing again. For example, I play the saxophone. The sax is a complex instrument with lots of buttons and springs and levers. As a result, things can go wrong with the sax that will cause it to play the wrong note. Periodically, when I play the note C-sharp, my sax suddenly and unexpectedly plays very flat. Because I have owned this horn for a number of years, I know that this happens, because a pad covering a valve near the neck of the saxophone has gotten stuck to the valve, and it needs to be opened. I do not need to think about how to fix this problem, because I can retrieve the solution from memory.

The first time that I had this problem, though, I needed to use more general causal knowledge about the way saxophones work. When I first started learning to play the sax, I learned that when a note on the instrument did not sound right, then there is often a problem with the horn itself (as opposed to a problem with the player). Some of the sour notes were caused by pads sticking to valves. Some problems were caused by springs that were not pushing the keys to their proper resting place. Still others were caused by loose screws. When I encountered the flat C-sharp for the first time, I checked the springs and pads, knowing that they can cause problems with the sound. Eventually, I found the pad that was sticking and pulled it off the valve. So, I used my rudimentary causal knowledge to help me solve a new problem.

The deeper my causal knowledge, of course, the more complex the problems that I can solve. In the case of the saxophone, my causal knowledge does not extend beyond knowing that pads can stick, springs can be too weak to hold up valve covers, and screws can come loose. I have a few solutions that people have taught me for helping prevent pads from sticking (like rubbing a dollar bill between the pad on the valve cover and the valve), but I do not have a deep causal understanding of the way the instrument works. If something more serious goes wrong, I have to bring it to a repair shop, where someone with more knowledge about the instrument can diagnose the problem and fix it. The people at the repair shop are experts in musical instruments.

When we classify someone as an expert, there are usually two dimensions of expertise that are important.

First, experts have skills (or habits) that allow them to perform actions that a nonexpert cannot perform. Experts in saxophone repair know how to remove the pads on the valve covers and replace them. They also have specialized tools that they can use such as lights they can stick in the horn to help them find leaks. Through practice, these experts become highly skilled at all of the actions involved in this kind of repair.

Second, experts have deeper causal knowledge than nonexperts. An expert in saxophone repair can diagnose problems by relating the symptoms of a problem to the factors that cause them. Then, the expert can use this causal knowledge to suggest a way to fix the problem. We value this type of expertise (and pay people for it), because this causal knowledge provides new avenues for solving difficult problems.

The two key elements of causal knowledge—that there are multiple explanations for the same event and that causal knowledge is nested—explain why it is so difficult to develop extensive causal knowledge. An expert must know about the many types of explanations that relate to her domain of expertise, and the expert must have knowledge of many of the nested levels of explanation that are part of that domain. Because of the volume of knowledge that must be acquired, it is impossible for someone to be an expert in every area.

Indeed, even within experts, there seems to be a trade-off between generality and depth of knowledge. In the medical profession, every doctor is an expert in medicine to some degree (compared to people who are not doctors). However, some doctors have a general expertise. Your doctor knows a lot about the many common complaints that people are likely to have most often when going to see the doctor. This doctor can give you advice for medical complaints ranging from the flu to minor injuries and skin ailments.

Every once in a while, though, a patient comes along with a rare condition. These rare conditions require specific causal knowledge to be treated effectively. A general practitioner will send this patient to a specialist to get the benefit of additional causal knowledge about a particular disease. This specialist knows a lot about a particular disease but probably has less general expertise than a family practitioner.

So, causal knowledge is a crucial part of your ability to solve new problems. If you understand why something works, then you can use that information to determine what has gone wrong when you are surprised at some outcome. This causal knowledge is also useful for suggesting ways to fix these problems.

Expertise consists of both skills that relate to solving problems as well as causal knowledge that goes beyond the norm. Causal knowledge is a crucial part of what allows experts to solve problems that baffle nonexperts.

Putting all of this together, then, causal knowledge is exactly the kind of High-Quality Knowledge you need for Smart Thinking.

instantly smarter
Leveraging the Expertise around You

You have probably heard it said that it is important to know what you know and to know what you don't know. As it turns out, it is also important to know who knows what you don't know.

From a young age, of course, we begin to discover that different people are likely to have a range of types of expertise. The research of Frank Keil and his colleagues demonstrates that even five-year-olds believe that someone who knows how refrigerators work is more likely to know how stoves work than to know what makes people happy or sad.

If you want to be smart, you clearly want to improve the quality of your own knowledge. In addition, you want to make sure that you know whom to call when you reach the limits of your knowledge. Spend time paying attention to which people you encounter who seem to have important knowledge that you are lacking. Use those people as resources to help you extend what you know.

The Illusion of Explanatory Depth

So how good is your causal knowledge? Think back to the many exams and tests that you have taken in your life. You have probably done well on a lot of them. But they don't always go well. The worst feeling is when you walk into an exam justifiably worried about your prospects for a good grade. Maybe you didn't have much time to study or you just couldn't motivate yourself to prepare for the test. Perhaps you studied hard, but felt like there were key concepts that still eluded your grasp. You walked into the exam concerned that you might not pass, and those fears were justified.

But sometimes, you may have walked into an exam with confidence. You felt like you really did understand the material that was being tested. You even felt confident after reading the first question on the exam. You thought you could give a good answer. As you started working out the answer you wanted to give, though, you discovered that you did not understand the concept being tested as clearly as you thought you did. Despite your high confidence, the knowledge you needed for the exam wasn't there. By the middle of the exam, your hopes fell. And by the end, you realized that you did not know the material at all.

How could this be?

This kind of experience reflects an important aspect of causal knowledge. Your judgments of confidence in your ability to explain things are not always that accurate. You shouldn't take my word for it, though. Let's try a simple exercise.

Take a look at this list of common objects. For each one of them, think about how much you believe you know about how they work. If you have a pen or pencil handy, write a number between 1 and 7 next to the object, with 1 meaning "I don't know at all," and 7 meaning "I know exactly how it works in great detail."

How a greenhouse works	
How a car ignition system starts the engine	
How a photocopier makes copies	
How a transistor works	
How a quartz watch keeps time	
How a flush toilet operates	
How a zipper works	
How a sewing machine works	
How a spray-bottle sprays liquids	
How piano keys make sounds	
How a ballpoint pen writes	
How a radio receiver works	

Is there an item here that you are pretty convinced you understand and could explain? If not, take a look around your house or the place where you are right now and find something that you are pretty convinced you could explain to someone else.

Now, I want you actually to explain how it works. If you have a sheet of paper handy, try to write down an explanation. If you don't, just try to give an explanation in your head. Start with the first step and carry through the chain of causal connections from one step to the next until you get to the last step in how it works. Try to tell as complete a story as you can without leaving any gaps. If you find that your story has a gap in it, then write the word *gap* in your explanation.

After you write out your explanation, go back and read it. Take a hard objective look at your explanation. How did you do?

Were there any gaps in your explanation? Were there places where you felt like you were not sure about how some of the elements are connected together? Were you surprised about the gaps in your causal knowledge?

If you found some gaps in your own causal knowledge, then you are not alone. Yale psychology professor Frank Keil and his graduate student Leonid Rosenblit conducted a study with college students very much like what you just did. They first asked people to judge how much they knew about a number of different devices. Then they had people generate explanations for devices that they thought they understood.

The central finding of this research was that there were many devices that people believed they understood but really did not. They expressed confidence in their ability to explain the way it worked, but when they actually had to produce that explanation, they failed. Rosenblit and Keil call this difference between people's belief about the quality of their causal knowledge and their actual ability to formulate an explanation the *illusion of explanatory depth*.

I'll give an example of a place where I found gaps in my own causal knowledge. When I first read about studies looking at people's causal knowledge, I tried it on myself. I started by attempting to explain how a flush toilet works. After all, I have fond memories of pulling the top off the toilet tank as a kid and flushing the toilet repeatedly to watch the mechanism work (until my parents would come by to tell me to stop). Surely, after all that time spent playing with the toilet I could explain how it functions.

I clearly understood some of the mechanism. The handle of the toilet is connected to a chain that pulls up a stopper at the bottom of the tank. That stopper is on a hinge. When the stopper is removed from the valve, the water in the tank starts to flow out. When all of the water has left the tank, the stopper no longer floats, and it falls down to cover the valve. When the water leaves the tank, a floating ball sinks with the water level turning on a switch that causes fresh water to start filling the tank. The water continues to fill the tank until the floating ball rises high enough to turn off the switch.

So far, so good.

But, where did the water go? For all of the time I spent watching the water leave the toilet tank, I never took apart a toilet to see where it went after it flowed out. That was the first gap in my knowledge. Somehow, the water left the tank and got into the toilet bowl. The second gap in my knowledge was that I had no idea why the water left the bowl. When the water level in the bowl gets high enough, it exits the bowl. Not all of it leaves the bowl, though, some of it remains. Why this happens, though, was a mystery to me.

My experience with this task is pretty common. Clearly, I fell prey to the illusion of explanatory depth.

Why does this happen?

When you are asked whether you know how something works, you do not generate a complete explanation for it before answering. Instead, you use some shortcuts to make this judgment. First, you try to imagine the mechanism at work. So if you can form an image in your mind of the device at work, your confidence that you can explain it will increase. Of course, if there are key elements of the process that are hidden from view (like how the water goes into the toilet bowl), then these elements will often be accompanied by a gap in your causal knowledge.

Second, as we talked about earlier in this chapter, explanations are nested. When you try to decide whether you can explain something, you try to retrieve some of the explanation. You assume that if you can retrieve some of it, then the rest will follow. However, sometimes you have a very general explanation without any more specific knowledge underlying it. I know that the water leaves the toilet tank and somehow gets to the bowl, but I don't know the mechanism that carries the water from the tank to the bowl and distributes it. This gap is evident only when I try to unpack my whole explanation of the toilet.

Indeed, many products are designed in a way that enhances this illusion of explanatory depth. I mentioned earlier that the Dyson vacuum uses clear plastic to give the user a view of the vacuum in operation. Being able to see the vacuum running is like staring at the toilet tank as the water drains out. The image of the swirling air provides the illusion of understanding. However, the principles of an industrial cyclone are complex, and just seeing it in operation is not enough to be able to understand how it works.

When you hear about the illusion of explanatory depth, you might think that your beliefs about the accuracy of any kind of complex knowledge are flawed. However, you have lots of kinds of complex knowledge for which you are quite accurate at judging the state of your knowledge. For example, you are generally quite accurate judging whether you know the plots of movies, books, and stories. They are complex, but if you believe you know the plot, you generally do.

Consider a number of stories you may have heard—*Romeo and Juliet*, *Moby-Dick*, *Finding Nemo*, *War of the Worlds*, *The Brothers Karamazov*. Some of these stories may be ones you think you know well, like *Romeo and Juliet* or *Finding Nemo*. Others you may know only vaguely. Others, you may not know at all. If you think you know the plot of *Romeo and Juliet*, then you probably do. You start with the duel between rivals, proceed through the meeting of Romeo and Juliet, the famous tower scene, and end with the tragic suicides.

The big difference between plots and causal knowledge is that plots are linear, while causal knowledge is nested. In a plot, each event leads to the next, so if you can remember the start of a story, you can generally be reminded of each subsequent event until you have retold the story. In contrast, causal knowledge is nested. So, even if you are able to remember part of the causal explanation, it is possible that you will not have elements of the causal knowledge underlying the initial explanation.

Even though plots may be complex there is no illusion of plot recollection. If you think you know the plot, then you probably do. If you think you do not know the plot, you probably don't.

Fixing the Illusion of Explanatory Depth through Specific Thinking

It is possible to improve your judgments about the quality of your causal knowledge by thinking specifically. At any given moment, you have lots of options for how you think about things in the world. You can think about your vacuum as a Dyson DC25. If you do, you are thinking about a particular model, so you are being quite specific. You could also think about vacuums in general. You could even think very abstractly and consider your vacuum to be a cleaning device.

Yaacov Trope and Nira Liberman are researchers who suggest that you can vary your level of *construal*, a term psychologists use to describe how a person perceives, comprehends, and interprets the world. That is, you can generate a mind-set to think about things specifically or abstractly. There are lots of ways to affect whether you will end up in an abstract or a specific mind-set. One easy way to influence your level of construal is to change your sense of how far away something is from you in space or time.

As an example, I am often asked to travel for work. Usually, I get an email or phone call several months before the trip asking me to give a talk or go to a conference. Because the trip is months away, I tend to think about it abstractly. I focus on issues like whether the conference will have interesting people at it or the location is one that would be enjoyable to see. After I agree to go on the trip, I put it on my calendar. As the date creeps closer, more specific issues start to arise. I have to reschedule meetings to accommodate the trip. I have to arrange things with my family to make sure the kids get to school. I begin to wonder why I am going on this trip at all, given how busy my schedule is.

None of these *specific* issues associated with my trip should have been a surprise, though. On any day of the week, I have meetings and family obligations. The obligations that I have today won't be that much different from the ones I will have a few months in the future. Because dates that are far off in the future are distant from me, they don't come readily to mind, and so they are less likely to influence my decision to go on the trip than the more abstract factors.

The same thing holds true for objects that are close to you in space. When you are far from your vacuum, then you are likely to think about it mostly as a device that helps you clean the floors. When it is right next to you, then you have to think about the weight of the vacuum, the location of the buttons, and the method for emptying the dirt out of it. Those details are generally more relevant when you are close to your vacuum than when you are far away.

When you have to make a judgment about whether you know how some object works, though, you are often far away from it. Right now, reading this book, your vacuum is probably tucked safely away in a closet. And you may not be anywhere near that closet right now. As a result, the situation promotes an abstract construal of a vacuum.

When you think about an object abstractly, the illusion of explanatory depth is particularly strong. You get a general mental image of some object and make a judgment about whether you understand how it works. When you think about an object really concretely, though, you are more likely to realize aspects of it that you don't understand. That means that if you have to make a judgment about whether you have a causal understanding of an object, you should try to imagine that object as being right next to you. By thinking about it specifically, you will make your judgments about the quality of your causal knowledge more accurate.

FILLING IN THE GAPS

Of course, that solves only part of the problem. Your causal knowledge still has lots of gaps in it. How can you work to minimize those gaps? Since High-Quality Knowledge is crucial for Smart Thinking, knowing that you have gaps is a good start, but those missing pieces will hinder your ability to solve new problems.

The main method for ensuring that you have high-quality causal knowledge is to learn a lesson from teaching. There is an old saying in education that the best way to learn something is to teach it to someone else. Indeed, a cornerstone of medical education is: See one. Do one. Teach one. The idea is that when a doctor is learning a procedure, she first needs to watch someone else carry it out. That gives her a general idea of how it is done. Next, she practices the procedure until she can carry it out. The process of doing something helps reveal some of the elements of the procedure that she did not understand. Finally, teaching the procedure to someone else makes sure that she has enough knowledge to really understand how the procedure is done and why it is performed.

The reason why teaching is so effective at helping you learn is that when you teach something to someone else, you have to form a complete and understandable explanation of it.

Both the words *complete* and *understandable* matter here. Complete seems obvious. If you get to a part of your explanation where you are not sure how to continue, then you have identified a gap.

Suppose you have to teach someone how a zipper works. You know that there are metal teeth in the zipper that are joined together and taken apart by the zipper mechanism. When asked to describe how the mechanism joins and separates the teeth, though, you may realize that you are not sure exactly how it works. Having to generate this complete explanation helps you find the gaps you have to fill in before you can effectively teach it to someone else.

Explanations also need to be understandable. Often when you give an explanation to someone else, you may use words whose meaning is not actually clear to you. In this case, you have given an explanation that appears to be complete, but it is actually not understandable either to you or to the person you are teaching.

Many years ago, I moved from Champaign, Illinois, where I was a graduate student to Skokie, Illinois, in preparation for my first job on the faculty at Northwestern University, which is located just north of Chicago. When I moved out of my apartment in Champaign, someone at the apartment complex told me that I would get my security deposit back soon. After several weeks went by, I called the apartment complex to find out why I had not yet received a check for my security deposit. The receptionist who answered the phone put me on hold and checked with the manager. She got back on the phone and explained to me that my security deposit would be refunded after my apartment had been "released." Puzzled, I asked what it meant for an apartment to be released. She had to put me on hold again to ask the manager.

Clearly, then, the receptionist passed on an explanation that she herself did not understand. On the surface, the explanation seemed fine. Unfortunately, it had a word in it whose meaning was not at all clear. The receptionist had a gap in her causal knowledge, and it was passed on to me.

It is quite common to use words whose meanings are not completely clear. When describing how the Dyson vacuum works, you may say that an industrial cyclone uses centrifugal force to separate the particles from the air. At one level, this is a true statement. However, if you do not understand the structure of the cyclone or if you are not familiar with the physics of centrifugal force, then the explanation is not really understandable. In this case, the words in the explanation are papering over a gap in your causal knowledge.

If there are any gaps in your own causal knowledge, you will find them in the process of teaching. Because you have to ensure that your explanations are good ones, you will not only identify the gaps in your knowledge, you will also work to fill them by doing additional reading and exploration to learn the information that you are missing. After all, teaching requires you to have good explanations. In this way, teaching improves your causal knowledge.

TEACH YOURSELF

Of course, you don't actually need to be in front of a classroom to do all of that work. You can treat every topic you encounter as if you were preparing to teach it. As you read new material or hear it from someone else in a lecture, you should attempt to teach it to yourself.

These *self-explanations* will help you find gaps in your causal knowledge. Those elements that you can't explain are an invitation to do more reading or to ask additional questions to make sure that you learn and understand the missing causal knowledge. Even if you choose not to fill a particular gap in your knowledge, you still have a better sense of the quality of what you know. That is, you have a better sense of what you do and don't understand. Sometimes, it is just valuable to know the limits of your knowledge. I am still not entirely clear on how the water exits the toilet bowl, but at least I know that I don't know it.

This process of self-explanation is particularly useful when studying for exams. Many people study by rereading the material that is going to be tested and deciding whether that material feels familiar. The illusion of explanatory depth makes clear that an overall feeling of familiarity is not a good way of predicting whether you will be able to produce a good explanation later. If the exam you are taking is going to require you to give an explanation, then the best way to ensure that you can generate an explanation is to actually produce that explanation when studying.

There are big differences between people in how naturally they explain things to themselves when learning. Some people almost always explain things as they are reading or listening to a lecture or watching a TV show. Other people rarely explain things to themselves unless they are really prompted to do so.

To get a sense of whether you generally explain things to yourself when learning, try the following exercise when you have a chance: Take the list of objects from the demonstration of the illusion of explanatory depth (on page 105) and find one that you do not understand. This object should be one for which you do not think you could explain how it works to someone else. Now, type "How does a [object] work?" into a search engine like Google or Bing. Among the first set of links should be a website that gives a fairly good explanation of how that object works. Often there are good explanations for the way things work at websites such as Wikipedia or How Stuff Works (www.howstuffworks.com).

Read the explanation as you normally would when trying to understand something new.

When you finish reading, explain how the object works to yourself without looking back at the explanation.

How did you do?

If you were able to explain it back perfectly, then chances are you are already a person who explains things to yourself as you encounter new information.

If there are any gaps in your explanation or things you did not understand, go back and read the passage over again. Try to fill in the gaps based on the explanation you read.

If you could fill in the gaps using the text you downloaded, then chances are you could have done a better job of explaining the object to yourself when you first read the description.

Eventually, you may find that there are still gaps in your explanation, but you cannot improve your explanation from the information you are currently using. In that case, you have found a limitation in the particular text you are working from. When that happens, you'll need to find another explanation that helps you fill in the remaining gaps.

Try to continue this process until you are satisfied with the explanation you have given for this object.

MAKING A SMART HABIT OF SELF-EXPLANATION

Now, think about the process you just went through. Did it feel natural for you? Do you feel like you understand things you read to the point where you could generate a good explanation after reading it once? For most people, the answer to that question is no. It does not feel natural to explain things as you go along. You often need to read things many times before you feel like you can explain them back. That is perfectly normal, but it also means that you need to work to develop the habit of explaining things to yourself.

As you develop your own skills at generating explanations when learning, you can help other people to acquire this habit as well. The best way to do that is to get people to justify or explain their conclusions in meetings and learning situations. Often, we do not ask other people to explain their chain of reasoning when they present us with new information. Perhaps we feel that the explanation would take too much time. We assume that the person presenting information to us probably knows the full explanation that led to their conclusion. Sometimes, we are reluctant to indicate to people that we ourselves may not understand the reasoning behind someone's conclusion. We fear that by asking questions, we might betray a weakness in our own knowledge.

The illusion of explanatory depth suggests that people may often be missing key aspects of their causal knowledge. In this case, the gaps will come to light only when they are required to give explanations. In addition, when someone gives an explanation to you, you may discover that you understood their point less well than you thought at first. Getting that explanation may, in turn, reveal gaps in your own knowledge.

AN INVITATION TO LEARN

If you push people to explain their reasoning, you must treat the gaps in people's knowledge as invitations to learn more rather than as signs of weakness. That is, we all know people who ask questions in the hope of playing *gotcha* by exposing errors in someone's reasoning or gaps in their knowledge in a meeting. That won't help people become smarter, though, because it will discourage people from wanting to volunteer causal information in the future. Instead, it is important to see gaps in causal explanations as opportunities to learn.

This process of asking people to explain their conclusions and encouraging them to fill in the gaps in the explanations that arise from these questions promotes learning. In this way, you are doing your part to create a Culture of Smart that will help you better understand what the people around you know and will increase the quality and depth of the causal knowledge of your peers, coworkers, and associates. By asking people to explain their reasoning, then, you make yourself smarter and you make the people around you smarter as well.

The Takeaway

Causal knowledge, the knowledge you use to answer the question *why*, is crucial for solving new problems. It allows you to go beyond solutions you have encountered before by giving you information you need to diagnose problems and generate new methods for dealing with those problems. Causal explanations are a uniquely human ability that allows us to create more complex tools by understanding the goals that people have when they act and the way that tools help those goals to be achieved.

A key aspect of causal knowledge is that it is *nested*: every explanation has another one associated with it that provides more causal information about why that explanation is accurate.

Despite the importance of causal knowledge, you may be poorly calibrated about the quality of your own ability to generate explanations. There are likely to be many instances in which you think you understand how something works, but in fact there are significant *gaps* in your knowledge. You can minimize the influence of this illusion of explanatory depth on your judgments by trying to think about objects *specifically* rather than only *abstractly*.

The gaps in your causal knowledge hold you back from Smart Thinking, because they represent situations for which you do not have high-quality causal knowledge to help you solve new problems. In order to ensure that you have reliable causal knowledge, it is important to develop the habit of explaining things to yourself as you learn them. A good explanation is one that is free of gaps (*complete*) and is also *understandable*. You need to make sure you do not have elements of your causal explanations that use concepts whose meanings are fuzzy to you.

Explaining things to yourself is like *teaching yourself* as you go along. And you have to go through the full teaching process. Don't just start the explanation and then assume you know how it completes from there. By teaching yourself, you identify and fill the gaps in your causal knowledge.

Finally, you should *demand this level of explanation* from the people around you as well. In this way you can create a Culture of Smart, by promoting good thinking habits from your colleagues, coworkers, and friends—as well as from yourself.

FIVE

Making Comparisons and Applying Your Knowledge

Reusing past experience requires finding
similarities between past and present.

Analogies allow you to use
similarities from distant domains.

Retrieving a good analogy can be difficult,
but there are ways to improve it.

IN 1955, RAY KROC OPENED HIS FIRST MCDONALD'S
restaurant in Des Plaines, Illinois. He licensed a concept
originally created by the brothers Richard and Maurice McDonald
in California, who set up a system for helping people get their
food quickly when traveling. Rather than having a waitstaff, people ordered for themselves in the self-service and take-out style
that has become ubiquitous in fast-food restaurants across the
globe. By the end of 1963, Kroc had sold more than a billion hamburgers in his fast-growing chain of restaurants.

There are lots of reasons for the success of the McDonald's
chain, but one of them is found in the way people use their knowledge. By the late 1950s the expanding highway system in North
America allowed people to take car trips long distances away

from home. It was difficult to know where to eat on these trips. There were no smartphones with apps that could recommend restaurants in any town. The quality of roadside diners was variable, and depended on who happened to own them.

The McDonald's chain changed that equation. From the shape of the building to the menu board in the restaurant, every McDonald's looked like all the rest. That meant that no matter where you were, when you stepped into a McDonald's, you immediately knew what to expect. After you had been to a McDonald's once, you knew what items were going to be on the menu and how to order your food in every single McDonald's restaurant.

Whether Kroc knew it or not, he found a powerful way to tap into people's ability to use their knowledge. Before McDonald's, people could use only very general knowledge to figure out where to eat when on the road. They could use broad cues to make a guess about whether they were going to get a good meal. These cues are often only partially reliable. We all know of restaurants that have great food, even though the building looks like it is about to fall over. And there are lots of beautifully appointed restaurants that offer poor food and lackluster service. After McDonald's, people could walk into a new restaurant they had never been in before and just do what they did last time with the expectation of the same result.

Indeed, McDonald's was so successful, that it set off a competition among fast-food restaurants. What is fascinating about the many different chains of restaurants striving for your business is that they have adopted a common model of service. Whether you are buying burgers, tacos, chicken, egg rolls, or sandwiches, the basic model for getting your food is the same. You enter the restaurant, and stand in line in front of a bank of cash registers.

The menu is printed on signs above the cashiers. When you get to the front of the line, you place your order, pay, and receive your food on a tray. If you dine in the restaurant, you find a table, eat, and at the end of your meal, you bring your tray to a bin. This structure for the restaurant experience allows you to reuse your knowledge gleaned from eating at one fast-food restaurant in a new one, even if you have never been into one of those franchises before.

While this anecdote may seem unremarkable, it actually says a lot about the power of the thinking processes that enable you to Apply Your Knowledge. Your ability to reuse old knowledge in new situations is rooted in your capacity to find similarities between new experiences and ones that you have encountered in the past.

Applying Your Knowledge

Following the development of Smart Habits and the acquisition of High-Quality Knowledge, the third part of the Smart Thinking formula involves Applying the Knowledge that you have.

Your knowledge is made up of two distinct types of information: *objects* and *relations*. Think about a typical McDonald's restaurant. There are lots of objects there—hamburgers and French fries, cash registers, menus, employees, grills, trays, and tables. Generally speaking, the objects in a situation are the things that you can label with nouns when you talk about them.

If you knew about only the *objects* at a McDonald's, though, you would be missing something fundamental about your experience in the restaurant. You wouldn't know what to do there or where to go. You would have trouble thinking about why you perform each step of the various procedures you have to go through to order food, pay for it, eat it, and clean up.

Relations provide the information about the relationships among all of the objects in a setting. Relations are typically described with whole phrases in which one word (often a verb) states the relationship that holds among two or more other objects.

We learn many different kinds of relationships over a lifetime. Some of them are spatial relationships that tell us where objects are located. The observation that the menu is normally located *above* the cashier is an example of a spatial relationship. Your knowledge also contains relations that describe actions, like the diner *places* an order *by talking to* the cashier. Other knowledge focuses on relationships in time. You place the order *before* you get your food. Another crucial type of knowledge involves the causal relationships that were the focus of Chapter 4: You look at the menu *because* it tells you what food the restaurant serves.

The objects and relations in your knowledge allow you to determine how new situations are like ones you have encountered in the past. When you go to a McDonald's in a new city for a meal, you recognize many of the objects, including the Golden Arches on the sign, the uniforms worn by the employees, and the hamburgers being served. You probably recognize the spatial relationships among the objects as well. The cash registers are beyond the seating area. The menu board is above the registers.

All of this similarity between the new experience and your previous knowledge allows you to identify where you are and to figure out what to do. You can take your knowledge of the actions, the sequence of the actions, and the causal relationships to order a meal. The McDonald's chain is designed specifically so that all of the elements that work in one restaurant will work in the others as well.

One of the particularly powerful aspects of similarity, though, is that a new situation does not need to be identical to a previous situation in order to be able to Apply Your Knowledge. The countless other chains of fast-food restaurants change many of the objects (like the uniforms, logos, and even the food), but they maintain enough of the objects to make the experience feel familiar. The counters, menus, and rows of tables have a striking similarity across restaurants. In addition, many of the relationships stay the same: the layout, the order in which you carry out the various actions, and the causal reasons why you perform those actions. Thus, despite the differences among the chains, there are a lot of similarities that support your ability to reuse your knowledge from one situation to the next.

Finding Similarities

How does this process of finding similarities work? To get a better feel for your own ability to make comparisons, let's try a simple exercise I first used in an experiment I did with my graduate mentor, Dedre Gentner, a psychologist who now works at Northwestern University.

Grab a sheet of paper and fold it in half. If you can't write where you are right now, then you can try this one in your head.

On the top half of the sheet, take about a minute to list things that the following pair has in common:

hotel   motel

Now, try one more of these. On the bottom half of the sheet, take a minute to list the things that the following pair has in common:

magazine   kitten

Now, try something a little different. Turn the page over and on the top half of the sheet, list all of the *differences* between the following pair:

car   motorcycle

Finally, on the bottom half of the sheet, try one more. List the *differences* between the following pair:

eggplant   giraffe

Let's start by thinking about the way you listed commonalities of the pairs. The items in the first pair—a hotel and a motel—are much more similar than the second—a magazine and a kitten. You were probably able to list many more commonalities for hotel–motel than for magazine–kitten. That shouldn't be so surprising. A lot of what makes a pair similar is that they have a lot in common. To the extent you could come up with anything that magazines and kittens have in common, you probably had to think quite abstractly (such as they are both things or they are both items you might see in a house).

Your ability to find the commonalities in a pair acts as you might expect it would. Items that are similar share many characteristics and those that are dissimilar share fewer. You might expect that differences would act the opposite way. That is, pairs that are very dissimilar might have more differences than pairs that are very similar.

Let's look in more detail at what you did when listing differences.

A car and a motorcycle are similar; an eggplant and a giraffe are dissimilar. However, the pattern of differences you can find is more surprising. Pairs of similar items like car–motorcycle actually have many differences. In fact, you probably found it rather easy to list differences for this pair.

Let's look more carefully at the differences you find for similar and dissimilar pairs. For similar pairs, the many differences you list typically involve contrasting aspects of each option. For example, cars have four wheels and motorcycles have two wheels. Cars usually carry more passengers than motorcycles. Cars also have larger engines than motorcycles. Each of these differences involves *finding a point of commonality between the pair and then noticing that there is some difference related to this commonality*. That is, cars and motorcycles both have wheels, but they differ in the number of wheels. Cars and motorcycles both carry passengers, but they differ in the number typically carried. Because these differences depend on the way your knowledge about the concepts is matched up (what psychological theories call *alignment*), these differences are called *alignable differences*.

When finding the differences between dissimilar pairs like eggplant–giraffe, the experience is not at all like what happens when you think of differences for a pair of similar items. Your initial sense is that the pair is *very* different, but the actual differences of the pair don't seem easy to access. Eventually, you tend to list properties of one item that have no corresponding property in the other item. For example, you might say that you eat eggplants, and you don't eat giraffes. Or that giraffes have long necks and eggplants don't. Because these differences reflect that there is no good alignment between your knowledge of the two concepts, these differences are called *nonalignable differences*.

The pattern of commonalities and differences that you can list for similar and dissimilar pairs reveals something interesting about the way comparison works. Our cognitive system wants us to focus on information that is likely to be useful for thinking. The differences between similar things are often helpful to know. You distinguish between cars and motorcycles on the basis of the number of wheels. You decide whether a car or motorcycle is a more appropriate means of transportation based on factors like the number of passengers they carry, and their relative safety and gas mileage. So the alignable differences between things are often important.

If you focused on nonalignable differences, then you would be overwhelmed with differences, and most of them would not be useful for thinking about contexts in which dissimilar items occur. If you see a shopping mall and a traffic light together, it is much more likely that you need to think about the relationship between traffic lights and malls rather than the differences between these things as concepts. At a shopping mall, you might think about traffic flow without ever considering the many ways that shopping malls and traffic lights are dissimilar. The comparison process provides access to commonalities and differences of a pair only when those commonalities and differences are likely to be useful.

ARCHIMEDES: A CASE STUDY IN SIMILARITY

Archimedes, the Greek thinker from Syracuse who lived about 2,200 years ago, was a designer, engineer, and physicist. He was asked by the king to solve a difficult problem. The king ordered a crown for himself that was supposed to be constructed from pure gold. When the king received the crown, he was suspicious that it had actually been manufactured using gold and some other metal. He asked Archimedes to determine whether the crown was made from pure gold.

At one level, this should be an easy problem. Gold has a known density, so all Archimedes needed to do was to weigh the crown and determine its volume. If the density of the crown was the same as the density of gold, then the crown was made of gold.

The difficulty was that the crown was ornately designed, and so it was irregularly shaped. Archimedes was not permitted to damage the crown, so he couldn't melt it down or transform it into a more regular shape to calculate its volume. Archimedes was stumped.

While pondering this problem, Archimedes took a bath. As he stepped into the tub, the water level rose, spilling water over the side. Archimedes noticed that the deeper he sat in the tub, the more the water spilled out. Legend has it that he was so excited by this observation, he leaped out of the tub and ran into the streets naked screaming "Eureka!"

Why was Archimedes so excited about this observation? He was able to make a comparison between this situation and the problem he was trying to solve. As Archimedes lowered himself into the water, the volume of his body caused an equal amount of water to have to move out of his way. Ordinarily, it might be hard to see the change in the level of the water in a large tub, but because it was already full the water spilled out. Comparing this situation to the problem he was trying to solve, Archimedes recognized that his body was just an *alignable difference* with the crown. If the crown was dipped in water, he could measure its volume by determining how much water had to move out of the way of the crown. And once he knew the volume and the weight of the crown, he could calculate its density. The principle that Archimedes discovered is now called the Law of Displacement.

The power of comparisons is that they allow us to find parallels between two situations. Once we recognize that there is some similarity between those situations, we can then see whether the solution that works in one case will also work in another: Archimedes recognized the similarity between the king's crown and his own body, and people use their knowledge of one McDonald's restaurant to determine how to order and eat in other fast-food restaurants.

THE POWER OF COMPARISONS

Comparison is not just a tool for problem solving; it is one of the core thinking processes. We classify new things based on how similar they are to items we have encountered in the past. Our reactions to new people are often affected by our interactions with similar people we have met. Habits are also based on similarity.

We are likely to perform an action by habit when a new situation is similar to one in which the habit has applied before.

Comparisons also help you evaluate people, products, and performance. Television talent shows and sports competitions like figure skating promote these kinds of comparisons. The first performer sets a standard, and the next is compared to the first. This comparison highlights both the commonalities between performers as well as the alignable differences. Unique aspects of a new performance (nonalignable differences) will often tend to get less attention and emphasis than will aspects that correspond to elements of a previous performer.

Often, of course, we make comparisons among some set of items to distinguish them from each other. We contrast the singers in a talent show or the competitors in a figure skating competition to determine which one is best. Obviously, differences are most important for these contrasts. As a result, we tend to pay most attention to the differences among the various competitors, particularly the alignable differences.

This focus on commonalities and (particularly) alignable differences is also true for what you tend to notice and learn about new situations. That is, you can think about most of your experiences in the same way you evaluate singers at a talent show or skaters at a competition.

The first time you encounter a situation, you remember as much as you can about it, and it provides your standard for the next time you encounter a situation like it. The first time in your life that you go to an airport, you may feel a bit lost, because you do not know what to expect. The entire process is difficult and effortful, but this initial encounter with an airport sets your standard for what you think an airport should be.

The next time you go to an airport, you call to mind what you learned about that first airport. At this point, you compare aspects of the new airport to the one you visited before. This comparison process between the new airport and the stored knowledge of the old airport focuses you on the commonalities and the alignable differences between the two. You probably saw gates at the first airport, and you will notice that the second airport also has gates. You may also notice that the seating area for the gates at each airport is configured differently. However, the second airport that you go to may also have a monorail system for traveling to distant gates that the first one did not. Because this latter property is a unique or nonalignable difference with the first airport you encountered, you may not notice this aspect of the airport unless it is pointed out to you specifically.

Obviously, unique properties can be noticed, but they are noticed despite the comparison not because of it. That is, for people to really become aware of the nonalignable properties of a new situation, those properties must call attention to themselves. Sticking with airports for a moment, the United Airlines terminal at Chicago's O'Hare airport has a strange underground passageway with neon lights, mirrors, and dreamy music. This passageway is so striking that even if you have never seen anything like it before, you notice it. Likewise, a figure skater who introduces a new movement runs the risk that the judges will ignore it unless the move is so jaw-dropping that it calls attention to itself.

Comparisons focus you on the commonalities and alignable differences of the items being compared. The nonalignable differences, which are unique properties of items, tend not to be noticed or learned unless they are pointed out specially (or they are very prominent). This focus affects your perception of items that you are comparing and influences the way you Apply Your Knowledge to a new situation.

instantly smarter
Comparisons in Choice

When you make important choices, you often compare the options to each other as part of the process of helping you reach a decision. When choosing an apartment or buying a house, there is a lot of information to be considered. Each option is a different distance from work and from shopping. The neighborhoods are different. The options themselves differ in the number of rooms and the size of the kitchen. In addition, some options may have unique properties. A particular house might have an area in the attic set up as an art studio. Another might have a gazebo in the backyard.

These comparisons focus you on the alignable differences of the options rather than the nonalignable differences. This focus influences both what you are likely to remember about the options later as well as what you are likely to choose. Aspects of the options that are comparable or alignable will be better remembered and will play a greater role in choices than aspects that are nonalignable. This will happen even when the nonalignable aspects of the options are actually fairly important.

This might seem a little counterintuitive. When comparing a house with a pool to one without a pool, you might think that you could represent that as a house with zero pools. Strange as it may seem, though, a large number of studies suggests that you tend to give unique nonalignable properties less weight in the choice than you would if the feature had had some correspondence in the other option.

To ensure that you do not miss important properties in a choice, there are three things you can do:

- **Try to evaluate each of the options independently rather than comparing them.** Think about the option as a whole and focus on what it would be like to have it. If you are choosing a place to live, imagine yourself living in that place. Think about the commute, the living spaces, and your daily activities. Try to generate this evaluation without thinking specifically about the alternatives. Remember that once you have moved into a new home, only the house you bought (and not the ones you didn't) will be relevant to your life.

- **Be systematic about your choice.** When the choice is important, write down the various aspects of the options. By making some kind of table or chart, you help make sure that aspects of the options you might forget still have a chance to play a role in the decision.

- **Use your emotions.** It is tempting to make a distinction between rational choices based on reasons and emotional choices based on feelings. However, there is good reason to believe that your emotional system responds to aspects of choices that are hard to put into words. Trust your emotions in choices. If one of the options feels wrong, there is probably some merit to that feeling. Likewise, if one of the options feels particularly good, that feeling should be taken into account. You should still consider the specific features of the options, but don't discount your emotions just because you are not completely sure where they have come from.

This Is Like That, Only Different

Clearly similarity is a powerful thing, but what happens when you don't have any knowledge that is obviously relevant to the problem? This is the situation we created for mechanical engineering design students in an experiment I did with my colleagues

Kris Wood and Julie Linsey. We gave students a new problem to solve: Design a set of weights that people could travel with so they could work out while on the road.

None of the students in this study had ever tackled a problem like this, and they were unaware of any similar products.

By the end of the study, however, many of the design students found ways to solve this problem. For most of these solutions, the students were able to use their knowledge, but they had to find a way to incorporate knowledge that did not seem obviously relevant. The most common solution drew on their knowledge of air mattresses. An air mattress is stored away most of the time. When it is needed, it is inflated, and provides a (somewhat) comfortable place to sleep.

A similar solution can be adopted for travel weights. That is, the "weight" should be added only at the time that it is needed. In this case, water provides a good source of weight. The groups typically designed some kind of water weight, in which there were inflatable waterproof containers at each end of a bar. The weights could be filled at a campsite or hotel room and used to work out and then emptied, dried, and stored for travel.

Air mattresses and water weights are generally quite dissimilar. One is used to sleep on, while the other is used to work out. One is designed to be comfortable, while the other is designed to be heavy and balanced. Yet, the knowledge of air mattresses was clearly useful for designing the water weights. The students in this study were able to use their knowledge, because people have a remarkable ability to form and use *analogies* to solve problems.

HOW DO YOU USE YOUR PAST EXPERIENCE?

The essayist George Santayana is credited with the following quotation: "Those who do not remember the past are doomed to repeat it." To use the past, though, it is crucial to figure out *which elements of the past are important for understanding the present and future*, because the past does not repeat itself precisely.

The historians Ernest May and Yuen Foong Khong have both explored the way politicians drew from the past to make decisions. They focused their studies on the period between the end of World War II and the Vietnam War. Two examples from their work will help illustrate the power of analogies.

The Domino Theory as Analogy

In the 1950s, politicians in the United States began to view the spread of communism by drawing an analogy to dominoes. We are all familiar with the game that involves lining up a row of standing dominoes, pushing the first one in the row, and watching as the rest fall over in sequence.

When thinking about dominoes in a row, we have knowledge of both the objects and the relationships among them. The objects are the dominoes. We know their inherent properties: hard, rectangular black blocks decorated with colored dots. We also understand the spatial relationship that the dominoes are close enough so that when one falls, it will hit another. This spatial arrangement leads to the causal understanding that tipping the first domino will cause it to fall into the next and so on in a chain reaction. In this analogy, dominoes are better understood than countries. The better-known body of knowledge is called the *base domain* of the comparison.

This domain was applied to thinking about countries in Asia within the sphere of influence of the Soviet Union. Because this area of knowledge was less well understood than dominoes, it is called the *target domain* of the analogy. The idea was that communist forces arising within the Soviet Union would cause governments in the region to topple and be replaced by communist regimes. The more countries that fell, the more that other governments in the region would also be in danger of falling.

Our ability to use analogies is impressive because we can focus on the similarities in the two domains of knowledge without requiring that the objects being compared be similar. In the case of the analogy with dominoes, nobody expects a country to be rectangular or to be distinguished by colored dots. The key issue is only that forces from one government could cause the government of a country close by to fall.

This analogy had a significant influence on the way foreign policy in Southeast Asia was conducted after World War II. For example, in the buildup to the Korean War, communists in the north of Korea battled with an opposition in the south. If this conflict had been seen as a civil war within Korea, then the United Nations would have had to watch the battle from the sidelines, because the UN charter does not permit the organization to get involved in internal conflicts within a country. Because of the domino analogy, though, the conflict was seen as *an influence of forces from outside Korea on the country*. As a result, the UN allowed member countries to try to intervene, and that led to the Korean War.

Not only do analogies structure the way we think about a situation but they also influence the predictions we make about future outcomes, or the target domain. These predictions are called

analogical inferences because they are extensions of our knowledge
(that is, inferences) made on the basis of an analogy.

Was Vietnam Like Korea?

Another example of an analogy in politics came from the start of
the conflict in Vietnam in the early 1960s. At this time, it became
clear that the United States military would have to get involved.
Officials in the Kennedy administration debated about which aspects of recent history provided the best guide to understanding
what might happen in Vietnam. Some administration officials argued that the United States should look to a very similar situation
in which the French occupied Vietnam. Instead, the administration chose to think about the growing conflict in Vietnam as being
similar to the Korean War that was fought a decade earlier. So, the
Korean War formed the base domain to the target domain of the
situation in Vietnam.

One of the most difficult aspects of the Korean War was that
China came to the aid of the North Korean forces. China was
threatened by the troop buildup in South Korea, and so it sent its
own forces to aid the North Koreans.

Because Korea was used as an analogy to Vietnam, officials in
the Kennedy administration made the analogical inference that if
China felt threatened, then it might also support the communists
in Vietnam. To try to prevent China from feeling threatened, and
therefore getting involved in the conflict in Vietnam, the Kennedy
administration made the decision to build up troops in the region
slowly. This gradual escalation of forces in Vietnam has been
blamed in part for the difficulties the United States had in the region. In addition, historians have argued that Vietnam did not

have the same strategic importance as Korea, and so it is unlikely that China would have gotten involved in the conflict.

LESSONS FOR ANALOGY

These two examples demonstrate both the power and the potential pitfalls of using analogy. On the one hand, analogies provide a key way to structure how you think about a new arena of knowledge that you do not understand well. Indeed, the domino analogy was so persuasive, that it became a dominant way for people to think about the spread of communism in Southeast Asia. Furthermore, the analogy between the Korean War and Vietnam led to predictions about what might happen, which in turn influenced strategy in the region. Later analysis of this conflict suggests that the inference that China would get involved was reasonable to make but probably flawed. Analogy is a potent source of predictions, but these predictions need to be verified in some other way, because the analogy does not guarantee they will be true.

To use an analogy, though, it is crucial to have High-Quality Knowledge about the base domain. Causal knowledge is particularly important to good analogies. Thus the more you know about how and why things work the way they do (high-quality causal knowledge) the more likely you will be to draw good analogies from one arena of knowledge to another.

instantly smarter
Communicating with Analogies

Analogies provide ways to communicate concepts that would otherwise be hard to articulate. Analogies can be effective given the limits of our vocabulary. We have lots of words for objects (like *camera*), and descriptions of objects (like *compact* or *digital*). We have fewer words for causal knowledge. We describe actions with verbs (like John *took* a picture of the children). But when we want to describe the way things work, it can often be more difficult to do unless we know the complex and specialized vocabulary that experts have. Even if we have a basic understanding of the fundamental idea of taking a picture (by exposing film to light briefly) and developing those pictures (by first developing the film into a negative and then projecting that negative onto photosensitive paper), it can be difficult to describe this sequence and the reasons behind it.

A less cumbersome way to describe the actions and causal knowledge associated with a new domain is to use an analogy.

When digital cameras were first introduced in the 1990s, manufacturers needed to communicate to potential consumers about the product. They could have tried to explain the product in great detail, but that would require consumers to spend the time to learn about them and still the description might be confusing.

Alternatively, manufacturers could use analogies. A digital camera could be compared to a scanner, which would indicate to consumers that the image was going to be stored electronically and processed by computer. This comparison is an analogy, because scanners and digital cameras may basically operate in the same way but look different and are typically used for different purposes. But the analogy provides an efficient way to communicate.

Using analogies to communicate has one other benefit: When the listener hears the analogy, he or she has to do a little work to find the correspondences between the base and target domain and to understand what is being communicated. As I discuss in Chapter 6, the more effort you exert when you encounter new information, the more likely you are to remember it later. So, the effort involved in understanding the analogy makes it more memorable. In addition, people's preference for the product is enhanced by the feeling that they discovered something new about it on their own. Using an analogy in conversation makes the topic more memorable and better liked by the listener.

The Analogy Bottleneck

I am hardly the first person to propose that analogies can be important for solving new problems. In his book, *How to Solve It*, mathematician George Pólya suggested that if you are trying to solve a difficult problem, you should find another problem that you solved in the past that is similar to the new problem and reuse the solution. Pólya was basically saying that analogy is a really powerful way to solve problems.

Why don't we use analogies more often? To start to address this question, try to solve the following problem:

Dr. Lee had a problem. One of her patients suffered from a stomach tumor that was probably malignant. Unfortunately, it was situated in a place where it could not be removed surgically. Instead, radiation was the only alternative. There was a problem with the radiation as well. Radiation that was strong enough to kill the tumor would also kill the healthy tissue around it causing permanent damage that would endanger the patient's life. How could Dr. Lee treat the patient successfully?

Spend a little time thinking about this one.

How did you do?

If you solved the problem, that is fantastic. That would put you in rare company. This problem was developed by psychologist Karl Duncker to study insight. Research with this problem suggests that only about 1 in 10 people are likely to solve this problem the first time they see it.

If you are part of the 9 out of 10 people who are usually stumped by this problem, let me give you a hint. Turn back to Chapter 1 and reread the story about Keith Koh and his factory that starts on page 10.

Now, try to solve the problem again, but this time use that story as an analogy to help you solve the problem.

How did you do?

What you have just done is to participate in a version of a study that Keith Holyoak has done with colleagues Mary Gick and Kyunghee Koh. In a number of experiments using this method, they observe that most people find the story very helpful for solving this problem. When this story is placed next to the problem, people see the connection between the healthy tissue and the fragile glass surrounding the bulb immediately. The cancer is like the damaged filament. The solution is also similar. Just as weak laser beams should be aimed at the broken point of the filament, a number of weak rays of radiation can be aimed at the tumor from different directions. None of the individual beams are strong enough to kill the healthy tissue, but the combination of the radiation rays focused on the tumor are enough to kill it.

So, the story about Keith Koh is quite helpful for providing a solution to Dr. Lee's problem. But if you are like most people, when you first read this problem, you did not think of Keith Koh. Assuming you have been reading the book from the beginning, you encountered this story way back in Chapter 1. But now, even though that story would have been helpful for solving a new problem, you did not call it to mind.

This example tells us something very important about problem solving by analogy.

Even though analogies can be very helpful for solving problems, we often have difficulty retrieving the information we need from memory to make the analogy when we need it. That leaves us with a bit of a paradox. On the one hand, analogies are very useful for solving problems. On the other hand, we are often unable to retrieve a base domain that we know about when we need it.

This example highlights a key bottleneck in our formula for Smart Thinking: Applying Knowledge. We have talked about ways of developing Smart Habits and for ensuring that you have High-Quality Knowledge. Now, it's time to look for ways to draw on that knowledge from memory when you need it.

IMPROVING ACCESS TO BASE DOMAINS

The reason why relevant base domains are hard to extract from memory is related to the importance of Smart Habits in thinking. Most of your life is spent in a world in which the proper thing to do is the same thing you did when you were in a nearly identical situation in the past. When you go to a McDonald's restaurant with the aim of getting a meal, you should stand in line, wait your turn, and order just as you have in the past. There is no need to be reminded of anything else other than previous trips to a McDonald's. When you drive home from work, you do not need to think about the fact that transportation systems and traffic bear some similarities to the flow of electrons through a wire. All you need to do is remember the turns to take at each intersection to get yourself home.

In general, then, you live in a world of literal similarity.

In fact, in many situations it would be delusional to start off by being reminded of things primarily from other domains. If Dr. Lee came to treat me for a disease, I would want her to think about her extensive medical training and to focus her treatment decisions on her knowledge of medicine. In general, I would not want her to start by thinking about treatment options that are based on ways that someone once fixed a lightbulb. I would only want her to start thinking about such far-flung solutions when her knowledge from within the medical domain had failed her.

Thus we are strongly biased to pull things from memory when they share both objects and relations with the current situation. For instance, the first time you walk into a new fast-food restaurant, you will easily call to mind other fast-food restaurants you have visited.

So, how can you improve your ability to use analogy to solve problems by pulling potential base domains from memory?

To get some insight into this process, think about proverbs. Proverbs are pithy ways to express some deeper wisdom. Start with a proverb you may never have heard before: "The noise of the wheels does not measure the load in the wagon." When you hear this proverb, what does it remind you of?

In my classes, when I ask students this question, the first answer I usually get is another proverb: "The squeaky wheel gets the grease." Both of these proverbs have wheels in them. However, they don't have the same meaning at all. But this kind of reaction is not unexpected since the mind jumps immediately to something else with *similar objects*.

The real meaning of a proverb is not focused on the objects in a proverb (in this case wheels and wagons), but rather on some set of relationships that could hold among many objects. This aspect of a proverb is its *relational meaning*. Think about the relational meaning of the proverb: "The noise of the wheels does not measure the load in the wagon." It refers to the idea that the inner essence of an object is not always reflected in its most obvious properties. This meaning is relational, because it describes the relationship between the inner essence of the object and its surface.

This relational meaning is also the key to allowing yourself to be reminded of proverbs that mean the same thing. Once you express the essential meaning of the proverb in this more abstract way, other proverbs that now come to mind will include "All that glitters is not gold," or "You cannot judge a book by its cover." These proverbs do not share any objects with the original, but they do mean the same thing.

The strategy of redescribing problems to find their relational aspects is crucial for allowing you to pull good analogies from memory. It is one of the best ways of Applying Knowledge.

You need to create a Smart Habit to take a new situation and focus on its relational meaning rather than focusing primarily on the objects. To help you do that, begin with some basic practice with proverbs. To get you started, give each of the following proverbs a relational definition (rephrase it in a more abstract way) and then think about other situations that come to mind. For example, the essence of the proverb "One cannot play all instruments in the band" can be expressed as "It takes individuals with different skills to do anything important."

A calm sea does not make a skilled sailor.

Sweep the snow on your own porch before you brush the frost from mine.

Put too much in a bag and it breaks.

Flies come to feasts unasked.

Great oaks from little acorns grow.

If a son is uneducated, his father is to blame.

It is a silly fish that is caught twice with the same bait.

You catch more flies with honey than with vinegar.

One man's meat is another man's poison.

One should be satisfied with beer when the wine is gone.

To create a habit of thinking about the essence of situations, you might want to try more than just the preceding ten proverbs. If you type "list of proverbs" into a search engine, you will find a number of websites with many more examples that you can use to hone your relational description skills.

After you have done this for a while, the proverbs have a second benefit. You will probably find a few proverbs that express the essence of problems you have encountered in the past. You can use the proverb to communicate that essence to someone else. Perhaps more important, using a proverb as a description of a problem may help you recognize new situations that share this essence in the future.

To see how useful proverbs can be for recognizing relational essences, I'll relate a story I heard from a colleague named Susan who was the editor of a scientific journal for many years. Scientific journals are rooted in a process of peer review. Authors send a paper to the journal, and it is sent to about three other scientists who are experts in the field. The paper is read carefully, and each scientist prepares a review of the work. The editor takes the reviews and makes a decision about whether the paper can be published. An important part of the review process is that the scientists reading the paper make suggestions that may improve the research. Often, the reviewers may actually suggest new studies that should be done before the paper will be ready to appear in the journal.

Susan and I were talking about the difficulty of being an editor. The identity of the reviewers is usually kept hidden from the authors of the paper. Some scientists have been known to write harshly worded reviews under the cover of this anonymity. Susan found that authors getting these reviews would often ignore suggestions made in the nasty reviews, even when the suggestions were good ones. At one point, she was reading a magazine article, and she came across the proverb, "You catch more flies with honey than vinegar." She realized that this proverb captured perfectly the problem she was seeing with these very negative reviews. Soon afterward, when she encountered a new review that was nastily written, she sent it back to the reviewer and asked for the review to be rewritten. She included the proverb as a simple way to communicate the reason why the review should be redone.

So far, this example just shows that proverbs can help you communicate a relational meaning that might be difficult to state literally. Susan went on to say, though, that after she started using this proverb, she started noticing lots of different situations in which it seemed to apply. When she had to criticize something her kids were doing, she started complimenting them first for something they had done and found that made them more willing to listen. She also began to notice how often her conversations with colleagues centered on sharing negative gossip. She began to focus on more of the positive achievements of her coworkers instead, and found that improved her relationships at work. What started out as a way of thinking about reviews at her journal had a transformative effect on the way that she interacted with other people.

The key idea here is that proverbs are one way to help you *categorize* new situations based on a relational essence rather than based on the objects that are involved in the situation.

CREATING RELATIONAL CATEGORIES

Using your knowledge requires that you recognize that some new thing should be treated similarly to something you encountered in the past. Most of the things in our world that we categorize are objects. If you walk into a hotel room after checking in, you quickly recognize the bed, chairs, and desk. Once you categorize the object properly, you know what to do with it.

Part of what makes objects so easy to categorize for people is that we have words that refer to those categories. Chairs may come in all shapes and sizes. Some have wheels. Some are comfortable. Some are big and bulky. Some can be folded and carried in a pouch. Having a word that we use to label the category helps us recognize new examples of that category when we encounter them again in the future.

Smart Thinking involves using analogies to Apply Your Knowledge. To make you more effective at recognizing potential analogies, it would be great if you had categories that applied to different situations that were all analogous rather than to different objects. Unfortunately, while the language (or languages) you speak provide you with lots of words for objects, language provides very few words that name the relational similarities that are shared by different situations that are analogous.

So, you have to create those labels yourself.

One way to do that is to use proverbs. Susan became skilled at recognizing new cases that were analogous to reviewers having their suggestions ignored when their reviews were negative by starting to apply the proverb "You can catch more flies with honey than with vinegar" as a label for the category.

There are many other ways that you could create labels for categories of analogous situations. For each, the key is to find something that provides an effective description of the basis of the analogy.

I started this section by pointing out that languages have few words for categories of analogous situations. You probably do have a few such labels, though, and you should create the Smart Habit to use them now that you know why they are helpful. Return to the case of Dr. Lee and her patient with the inoperable tumor: Dr. Lee wanted to damage unhealthy tissue without harming the healthy tissue surrounding the tumor. The idea of destroying a target without harming nontargets brings to mind the term *collateral damage*. Collateral damage started as a military term to refer to the destruction of nonmilitary targets during military operations.

Oncologists like Dr. Lee are trying to avoid collateral damage. This term provides a label that captures a relationship that can apply across many different domains. In addition to the military and oncology, another domain in which you want to avoid collateral damage is weed killing. When trying to kill weeds in a lawn, you want to remove the unwanted plants while preserving the desired grass. Yet another domain where collateral damage comes up is painting the ceiling. When you paint a ceiling, you want to get the paint on the ceiling, but not on the walls, floor, and furniture. Once you have recognized the similarities among these domains, you can explore ways that solutions to the problem of collateral damage in one domain might be transferred to another.

Story titles and joke punch lines can also be used as relational labels. Stories and jokes encapsulate a set of relationships among characters. It would be cumbersome to have to retell the story or joke every time you wanted to think about those relationships, but the title of the story or the punch line of the joke can be used as a label that refers to the whole thing.

Aesop's fables are often used in this way, because the stories were written to capture a particular relational truth. Here's a version of one classic story:

A hungry fox was walking through the forest trying to find something to eat. He saw some grapes hanging on a vine in a farmer's yard and stood beneath them. He jumped at them for a while, but even the lowest-hanging bunch was beyond his reach. Finally, he looked at them in disgust and said, "Those grapes are not ripe yet anyhow. I don't want any sour grapes."

From this fable, the term *sour grapes* refers to a situation in which someone does not get what he wants, and so he devalues the former object of desire. As I discussed earlier, it is fairly easy for people to recall the story line of a movie once they get a few key plot points. That is what makes stories a good repository for relational knowledge. Giving the story a title (like "Sour Grapes") provides an easy way to refer to that story later.

Stories can also be built directly into a teaching system, such as that used by Harvard Business School. Classes are structured so that lessons are taught by working through real case studies (stories) of businesses in which particular problems had to be solved. Each case incorporates a lot of detail. Students are expected to learn the details and to work both as individuals and in groups to make real decisions about how to proceed. In the classroom, the professor leads discussions among the students to explore options for how to deal with the case and to draw lessons from it.

There are many benefits of the case study method for Smart Thinking. For one, students are forced to explain many of the details of the case to themselves. In addition, because they may have to talk about it extensively in class, they have to be prepared to teach their reasoning to others. As a result, they are likely to emerge from a case with a deep understanding of how and why things worked in a complex situation.

In the end, the business associated with the case becomes a label for the set of relations that are relevant for that business situation. The exact situation described by a case studied by business school students may never come up again. What makes these case studies effective is that students learn to recognize the key causal elements that made a particular solution effective. Giving the case a label then helps students categorize new problems they encounter as additional examples of the case they first saw in class.

Another method for describing relational systems that can create relational labels is to use the punch lines of jokes. Jokes are effective, because a good joke is usually designed to be brief and

easy to understand, but a joke is often funny because it also captures some deep truth about the world. Consider the following
joke:

> A woman brings her young son to the beach where he plays con-
> tentedly in the sand. Suddenly, a huge wave comes and washes
> him into the ocean. Distraught, the woman looks at the heavens
> and says, "Please, bring my baby back! I'll do anything. Please!"
> A moment later, a second wave breaks on the beach, depositing
> the baby on the beach completely unharmed. The woman looks
> at the baby, and then back at the heavens and says, "He had
> a hat!"

I often use the phrase, "He had a hat" to refer to any situation
in which someone is complaining when he ought to be grateful.
The punch line serves as the label that stands in for the rest of the
joke. Like story titles, proverbs, and relational labels, punch lines
help you recognize the basic elements of new situations.

The purpose of relational labels is to help you to think differently about a problem you are currently trying to solve. If you
focus on a problem only within the domain in which the problem
was originally stated, then you are generally going to draw on
your knowledge from that domain.

Using these techniques will take some practice and preparation. You may not know a lot of proverbs right now. You probably
have not thought about the various ways of giving labels to categories of problems that you have encountered. You may never
have thought of jokes as invitations to categorize situations. But
you can create Smart Habits if you become more mindful of the
way you choose to think about difficult problems.

The effort you put into finding new ways to think about problems will be rewarded in the improvements in how well you can think of analogous situations. It will take some time, but this is a surefire way to improve your ability of Applying Knowledge.

The Takeaway

Similarity and analogy are crucial for helping you Apply Your Knowledge. You draw on experiences that are very much like the one you are in right now to determine what to do next. You tend to focus on what the current situation has in common with previous situations as well as on the differences that are related to those common aspects. Unique (or nonalignable) elements are generally not emphasized in your thinking.

Your ability to find similarities between two situations is actually quite flexible. In addition to finding obvious similarities, you are skilled at making analogy comparisons that focus on the similarities between what you know (base domain) and what you don't know (target domain). While the *objects* in those domains need not be similar, analogies highlight the relational similarities and can be used to communicate information about the similarities, making the target domain easier to understand. These inferences by analogy have to be treated with caution, though, because they are not guaranteed to be true.

Although analogies are a powerful way to help you understand new situations, you often do not retrieve analogies that you know from memory. Information is usually drawn from memory based on the overall similarity of the new situation to something you encountered in the past. To focus retrieval on analogies, it is important to redescribe the problem to emphasize its essence and to deemphasize the objects. Using proverbs, relational category labels, story plots (or more prosaically, case studies), and even jokes helps make you smarter by improving your ability to Apply Knowledge to solve new problems.

SIX

Maximizing Memory Effectiveness

Getting information into memory
requires deep and active processing.

To change your thinking,
change what you are thinking about.

Use different modes of description
to help you change your thinking.

IT WOULD NOT BE A STRETCH TO SAY THAT AUGUSTE
Rodin's sculpture *The Thinker* is one of the most recognized statues in the world. There are copies in museums, in a number of public settings, and countless desktops.

The statue is notable, because it really depicts a physical struggle. Rodin himself originally intended the sculpture to be seated at the top of a project called *The Gates of Hell*. It was meant to show Dante planning his poem *The Divine Comedy*. Rodin was trying to find a way to capture the thinker as a creator. Art scholars comment on the physical effort that the statue brings out. For Rodin, complex thinking involved absorption of both mind and body.

I have always been struck by this sculpture, both because it really is a magnificent work of art and because it reflects a common view of thinking. It is typical to think that when someone is solving a difficult problem, she is working hard. There is some truth to that, of course. The brain is a very energy-hungry organ that makes up only about 2 percent of your body weight, but uses about 20 percent of the energy that your body consumes each day.

While your brain consumes a lot of energy, Smart Thinking certainly doesn't feel like the sort of intense physical labor that Rodin's statue implies. In fact, when you're trying to solve a hard problem, a sense of extreme physical effort is most likely a signal that you're doing something wrong.

Generally speaking, intense thinking feels pretty good. I remember difficult exams in college for which I spent three hours writing out the answers to a series of essay questions. I was certainly drained after organizing my thoughts and drawing together a semester's worth of learning. During the exam, though, I would experience what Mihaly Csikszentmihalyi calls *flow*. Each thought led seamlessly to the next one and I often lost track of time.

When thinking is not going well, then it may feel much more physically uncomfortable. Years ago, I was traveling to attend a conference in Sofia, Bulgaria. Through a series of mishaps, I ended up having to spend a night in Zurich, Switzerland. When I exited the Zurich airport, I immediately felt disconcerted. I do not speak German, so I couldn't read or understand many of the signs. But all was not lost. I still knew a lot about airports, and I made a guess about where I would find the shuttle bus, and sure enough, there were buses leaving. When I got to the hotel, I went out and found a building that looked like a bank and changed a little money for the day. I walked the streets for a while, enjoying the sights and, in the end, survived the experience. (Frankly, the Swiss are almost all multilingual and seemed willing to take pity on a stranded traveler, so it was not hard to get the information and directions I needed.)

But, I never felt really comfortable. During the entire episode in Zurich, I had some anxiety that I would not get back to the airport on time. I had to think about every aspect of the day. I would not say that I used my thinking faculties very productively or effectively—I felt a lot more like Rodin's thinker on that day than during any of the exams I took in college.

To understand the difference between my experiences in a foreign country and taking the exams for which I was well prepared, it is important to learn more about the way memory works.

Let's begin with an easy exercise. Try to remember a birthday party that you went to when you were a child.

How did you do?

Chances are as soon as I asked you to remember a birthday party, without any special effort, you retrieved this information from memory: the sights, sounds, and perhaps even emotions or smells. You may have conjured up images of the party itself with paper hats, balloons, a birthday cake, and perhaps a Pin the Tail on the Donkey game.

The memories you have involve a conscious recollection of a past experience. These conscious recollections are called *explicit memories*. There are two important observations we can make about explicit memory. The first is that recalling information from memory is effortless. If you are exposed to a piece of information (like the request to think about a birthday party from when you were a child), then you automatically bring to mind memories related to that information.

The second observation is that the information you call to mind is always related to what you are currently thinking about.

That is, you probably were not thinking about birthday parties when you started reading this chapter. But when I made you start thinking about birthday parties by mentioning them here, your memory obliged you by giving you some information about birthday parties.

However you may have had trouble pulling out a specific memory of a birthday party. In which case, just the words *birthday party* weren't enough to call one to mind. After that, though, you probably succeeded in thinking about a specific birthday party by changing the focus of what you were thinking about: You might have tried to imagine a cake or pointy hats or a game of Pin the Tail on the Donkey. One of those thoughts was then enough to trigger a memory from your childhood.

Now, let's try a second exercise. Try to remember a birthday party for an adult that you went to recently.

Again, you probably remembered something easily. But the information you pulled from memory was probably quite different from the party you recalled from your childhood. This party may have had a cake, but probably fewer party hats, different beverages, more conversation, and (I assume) fewer games of Pin the Tail on the Donkey.

A lot of times when people discuss memory for life events, they are interested in the accuracy of those memories. The information you recall about a birthday party from when you are a child could be an accurate memory of your experience. But it also might be a mixture of a few different parties you attended as a child. It might even have elements of things that you saw in home movies or videos of the party when you were older.

For the purposes of Smart Thinking, though, it doesn't really matter how accurately your memories reflect a particular event of your life. Your memory did not evolve to support an accurate playback of your life. Instead, it evolved to give you the information you are likely to need when you need it. If you were a hunter-gatherer living 10,000 years ago, you might be out with a group trying to bring back a meal for the group. When you reached a particular stream, you would call on all of your knowledge about how to proceed. That knowledge might include stories passed on by members of the group, your own experiences from prior hunts, and things you watched other people do in the past. The source of this information doesn't matter as much as your ability to use it to carry out this hunt successfully.

How Memory Works

The basic principle that determines what information is going to be retrieved from memory is straightforward: Information is retrieved from memory when the current situation matches the situation in which that information was learned.

The key word here is *situation*, which psychologists also call *context*. When you learn new information it becomes associated with the context in which you are learning—sights, sounds, tastes, smells, feelings, and even thoughts that were present at the time. Since your memory is built on the principle that knowledge is likely to be important when the same situation occurs again, your memory wants to give you the information that is most likely to be helpful for you. As we saw in Chapter 5's discussion of fast-food restaurants like McDonald's, your memory is designed so that when you walk into any McDonald's, you are reminded of other visits to McDonald's so that you can use your knowledge about those past visits to help you understand what you need to do to get a meal.

To explore the influence of this principle further, let's delve a bit into your own past. If you are like most people, you have not always lived in the same house or apartment. You probably have some memories of a childhood home. Just providing a simple cue like "childhood home" is likely to be enough to help you call to mind some memories. When you have some time, let your mind wander through your memories of that childhood home a bit. If you form a mental image of your bedroom, does that bring to mind even more information? The reason you remember even more once you start forming these mental images is that you are re-creating a little more of the mental context from when you used to live in that home, which allows you to remember additional aspects of that home. If you were able to get even more of the context, then you might remember things you had not thought of in years. Sitting down with your parents or siblings, looking at an old photo album, or even revisiting your childhood home would add sights, sounds, and even smells that may have been part of the original context of some of your early memories and thus might help you remember things from your past.

A classic psychology experiment demonstrates how rich the context for a memory can be. Duncan Godden and Alan Baddeley looked at memories formed in two different settings. The participants in the study were all trained scuba divers. The basic memories they formed in this study were not that interesting. They heard lists of words that they would have to remember later. Having to remember a list of words is similar to remembering things about a childhood home. Even though the words themselves may be familiar, what is important is that those particular words appeared on that particular list.

Participants were asked to learn some of the word lists while they were sitting on land near the water and the other lists while diving underwater in full scuba gear. In each case, the divers were listening to the lists using a scuba diver communication system. After a delay, participants were asked to recall the lists, either on land or in the water. To recall the words, they wrote on plastic boards with pencils that could be used either on land or in the water. In this study, the context is quite rich. Sitting by the water involves all sorts of sights, sounds, and smells that are distinctive to being near water. Underwater, the scuba divers had a very different context. They were breathing through an apparatus. They were surrounded by water pressure. They could feel the temperature of the water against them.

All of these contextual factors affected how well people could remember the words on the lists. When participants learned a list while sitting on land, they were better at remembering that list when they had to recall it *while on land* than while underwater. When they learned the list while diving, they were better at remembering the words on the list when they were tested while diving than when they were tested on land.

Most of the situations you have been in won't be quite as extreme as diving underwater with scuba gear on. Still, if there is something that you are trying to recall, then you can give yourself the best shot at remembering it by re-creating as much of the situation as possible from when you learned the information in the first place.

When you lose something, your ability to recall can be enhanced by mentally retracing your steps. I used to misplace my car
keys in the house frequently. Whenever that would happen, I
would start thinking back through the day from the time I got
home, and eventually I would remember where I had put them.
Visualizing each aspect of the day re-created more of the context
of those events, and let me remember where I had emptied my
pockets, which then allowed me to recall where I had set down my
keys. (Since then, I have instituted a Smart Habit. I put up hooks
by the garage door and have trained myself to always hang the
keys there.)

This core principle of memory makes it clear that using your
knowledge effectively requires getting High-Quality Knowledge
into your memory and then creating a context that is similar to the
one in which the memories for that knowledge were created. To
use your memory effectively, then, you have to influence both the
way you get knowledge into memory as well as the strategies you
use to help you get information out of memory.

Getting Knowledge In

The discussion of the Role of 3 in Chapter 3 and the influence of
self-explanation in Chapter 4 were both aimed at improving the
quality of your knowledge. What these two suggestions have in
common is that they require that you be an active learner. Making
sure you focus on the key points of an event after it is over involves doing some work to control what you are most likely to

remember and putting in effort to connect the important information to your existing knowledge. Self-explanation is also clearly an
active process. It requires that you generate explanations as you
go along to identify the gaps in your causal knowledge.

What this ought to make clear is that there is no magic trick for
acquiring High-Quality Knowledge. I am sure that if someone
could develop a technique for allowing you to learn without effort,
that person would be hailed as a hero and put on the front page of
every magazine. The publicity surrounding the Mozart effect is a
great example of our desire to get something for nothing.

The Mozart effect refers to the claim that listening to the music
of Mozart can lead to an increase in performance on cognitive
tasks. The popular interest in this effect came from some initial
studies suggesting that people who listen to Mozart (or other complex classical music) do improve temporarily when solving spatial
problems like mazes. This would seem to be a nearly perfect
tool for making you smarter. Listening to Mozart is enjoyable. It
doesn't require a lot of effort. Much like the exercise gadgets that
are advertised in magazines that claim to get you toned and fit in
just five minutes a day, the Mozart effect captured a lot of people's
attention. Companies were created to sell music that was designed
to increase your intelligence. Even former Georgia governor Zell
Miller proposed that the state should purchase classical music
CDs for every child born in the state in 1998.

Unfortunately, it doesn't look like listening to Mozart (or any
other music) will make you generally smarter or allow you to perform better on tests of thinking in general. Some of the effects of
listening to music seem to come about just because you tend to
perform better on tests of thinking ability when you are in a good

mood—and listening to fast tempo music will typically improve your mood. Any other effects of listening to music on thinking seem to be small and short-lived. Sorry.

DEEP THINKING

Getting High-Quality Information into your memory requires lots of hard work. You have to think about things deeply to get them into memory successfully. What does it mean to think deeply?

Take a moment and try to answer that question for yourself.

Did you stop and think about it when I asked you to or did you just read on? If you are just reading on, then you are hoping that I'll tell you the answer. You're right, of course, this whole section of this chapter is about ways to help you get more information into memory.

The problem is that if you simply read what is written here, you may not really store all of the information in memory. Psychologist Bob Bjork talks about this issue when he explores how we evaluate how well college professors teach. College professors don't generally have formal teaching evaluations done by peers like teachers in grade school. On occasion, we do ask one faculty member to sit in on the lectures given by another. That is done most often when someone is being evaluated for a promotion.

Most of the feedback that college professors get about their teaching comes from the students at the end of the semester. The students rate the course and the professor on a number of criteria and, in addition, offer general comments. These ratings are compiled and given to the faculty members. (There are even companies that run websites like Rate My Professors [www.ratemyprofessors

.com] where students can access these evaluations to find out more about who is teaching classes they may be considering.)

How effective are those evaluations in determining how much students actually learn? According to Bjork's analyses, students give high ratings to professors when there is humor in the lectures (so that they are enjoyable) and when the professor tells clear and understandable stories. That is, when the professor is fun and it is easy for students to get the point of the lecture, then students feel good when they leave class. It seems obvious that these qualities should improve a professor's rating. A lecturer who is well prepared and delivers the material clearly is helping make the course engaging for the students.

DESIRABLE DIFFICULTIES

It turns out, though, if the lectures are too clear, and the students in the class don't need to really think hard to follow the lectures, then they may not actually learn as much of the material as they would if they were challenged to teach themselves more of the material during class. These challenges create what Bjork calls *desirable difficulties*. That is, some hard work during learning may be frustrating, but it leads to better learning in the long run than a situation in which you do not have to work hard. Bjork suggests that the paradox of college course evaluations is that the factors that lead to good evaluations are not quite the ones that help the students maximize how much they learn in the class.

There is a lot of good evidence that supports the importance of desirable difficulties in learning. The more you think for yourself in a learning situation, the better your memory for that information. In experimental research, this improvement is called the *generation effect* because you are generating the information for yourself rather than just having that information presented to you by someone else. When you listen to a really fluent lecture, you do not have to do much work to connect the dots in what you are being told and so you may end up learning a lot less about the topic than if you had to work harder during learning

ACTIVE LEARNING

The generation effect works for a few reasons. First, generating information on your own ensures that you have actually understood the information that you are thinking about. That is the effect of self-explanations discussed in Chapter 4. The value of self-explanation is that it helps identify the gaps you have in your understanding of the way things work. By generating an explanation, you help guarantee that your knowledge has no gaps.

Second, generating information helps solidify the *connections across pieces of information*. Think of your knowledge as a pile of peanuts. If all of the pieces of your knowledge are independent, then it is like having a bunch of salted peanuts in a bowl. Picking up any one of them will not affect your chances of picking up another. Even if you try to pick up a bunch in your hand, there is always a chance a few will slip through your fingers. But if you pour caramel over the peanuts and let it harden, then you get peanut brittle. Now, picking up one peanut allows you to pick up all of the other ones stuck to it. Generating information provides the connections among ideas that allow them to be drawn out together.

Third, generating information for yourself reinforces the relationship between the information you are learning and the internal state of your memory. You encounter new information in a variety of situations. You might be reading or attending a lecture. Perhaps you tuned into a documentary on TV. If you are passive while learning, then most of the context that will be associated with the new knowledge involves the situation in which you are learning. If you watch a lecture passively, then the new knowledge you are gaining is most strongly associated with aspects of the scenario at that moment. The voice of the lecturer, the sounds and smells of the room, and even the temperature all become associated with what you are learning. When you need that information later, though, you probably will not be in the same setting.

When you learn actively and work to repeat key information and produce explanations for yourself, you create a rich mental context in which you are learning. This internal context consists of the thoughts you are having that relate to the material and the goals you have for learning about it. Even if you are in a very different location when you need the information, there may be many aspects of your internal context that are present when you need the information again. So processing information deeply helps you make the information more strongly associated with your internal mental context rather than with transient aspects of the outer world.

For all of these reasons, it is important to process information deeply when you are trying to learn it. This deep thought will create elaborate memory representations that can be used in future situations. The more elaborately you learn, and the more connections you make among components of your knowledge, the easier it will be to find situations later that cue that knowledge to be retrieved from memory.

LEARNING IS A MARATHON NOT A SPRINT

From the elite runners who plan to finish a 26.2-mile race in a little more than two hours to the recreational runners who may take four or five hours to complete the run, participants in a marathon all have one thing in common: Each of them has trained extensively for this difficult achievement. Solid marathon preparation requires months of training, and most runners will train at least four or five days a week. Nobody would seriously consider preparing for a marathon by trying to run a huge number of miles in the week before the event.

Often, however, we do not give the same level of preparation for acquiring High-Quality Knowledge. It is common for students in high school and college to cram, reading the material and answering all of the review questions the night before the exam. The results of this method are no more successful than trying to prepare for a marathon in a week.

For one thing, in many situations in which people are getting ready for an exam, students underestimate how long it will take them to prepare properly. It is hard to pack an entire semester's worth of studying into one night. But even if you had enough time, it is still less effective to jam all of your preparation into one last-minute study session than to spread it out over a longer period. When you study the material in one sitting, you end up associating all of that material with one context. The sights and sounds and smells and emotions that you are experiencing during that study session all become part of your memory for that knowledge. Unless you are in that same situation again, it will be difficult to retrieve what you have learned.

If you spread your studying out over a longer period of time, the knowledge becomes associated with many different contexts. When you learn material over several days or weeks, there will be many sights and sounds and smells and emotions across the many different times that you encounter the information you are learning. Even if you spend a lot of time learning new material while sitting at your desk or in a particular study carrel at the library, there is still a lot that will vary. You'll be wearing different clothes. You may be hungry one time and full at another. Your mood may be different as well. As a result, there are many different kinds of contexts that may help you remember that information again in the future.

Studying in a variety of settings also helps reinforce the connection between the material and your internal context. No matter what the physical environment in which you are studying, however, chances are that your internal context—your focus on what you are studying—will remain constant. So the more often you study the material, the better the chance that just one bit of the material becomes a trigger to remember the rest of it. So treating study like a marathon helps insulate your knowledge from extraneous factors like the physical environment in which you were studying.

Ultimately, High-Quality Knowledge is more than a set of facts. You will do a better job of building connections among the components of your knowledge when you study over time.

Change What You Are Thinking About

Apple computer had an advertising campaign that consisted of pictures of influential people along with the tagline "Think different." One reason why this ad was so popular is that it fits with a widely accepted idea that having amazing and revolutionary thoughts requires new modes of thinking. The popular phrase "thinking outside the box" also focuses on the idea that truly creative thinking must somehow go outside the prescribed lines.

How can you really think in a different manner? I mentioned earlier that successful thinking doesn't feel at all like physical exertion. Smart Thinking is not a strain. But what happens when you get stuck? At an impasse, you do feel frustrated. At that point, perhaps the mental heavy lifting begins.

As it turns out, the pathway out of every impasse starts with a white bear.

To see what I mean, for the next 30 seconds, whatever you do, don't think about white bears. Don't do it. Resist it.

How did you do? If you actively tried to prevent yourself from thinking about white bears, then you probably spent all 30 seconds thinking about nothing but white bears. *Memory retrieval is automatic.* You can't stop yourself from pulling information out of memory. It just happens.

The only way to avoid thinking about white bears for 30 seconds is to will yourself to start thinking about something else. Recite the lyrics to a song. Imagine a boat trip you went on. Look at an object in the room and try to explain to yourself how it works. Once you get on the road to thinking about something else in specific terms, you won't think about white bears anymore.

Just as you would try to direct your thinking to any subject except white bears, when you are stuck on a problem that you are trying to solve, you need to find a way to retrieve new knowledge from memory that might be relevant to that problem. The only way to get something new out of memory is to change the content of what you are thinking about at that moment. You need to change what you are using as a cue.

At its core, Smart Thinking does not require you to think differently but *to think about different things.*

To see this in action, let's return to the study I did with Kris Wood and Julie Linsey that I described in Chapter 5 in which engineering students had to design exercise weights that could be used while traveling. Ultimately, students in this study were able to draw an analogy between the weights and an air mattress. How were they able to do that?

Initially, the students tended to get stuck. They were unable to think of any particularly good designs. At that point, we encouraged them to think more specifically about the way weights are designed using a vocabulary of terms for functions that they learned in their engineering classes. This vocabulary includes methods to describe the items at the end of the bar as containers for weight rather than just cylinders of metal.

This new description helped participants in this study to see that a container for weight could be emptied in the same way that air mattresses are emptied, and that formed the basis of an analogy that ultimately led to the solution of creating exercise weights that could be filled with water.

There are two key components to this example. First, getting out of an impasse required changing the description of the problem to be reminded of new knowledge that might help solve the problem. Second, these students succeeded in part because they learned a specialized vocabulary that enabled them to describe the functions of the parts of the product they were designing.

instantly smarter
When Retrieval Feels Hard

A key premise in this chapter is that memory retrieval is effortless. But every rule has an exception. In the case of memory, this exception is best seen through the lens of Trivial Pursuit, a board game invented by Canadians Chris Haney and Scott Abbott. This game involves answering questions involving general knowledge and popular culture.

There are three kinds of responses that people have to questions in the game. One, they just *know* the answer to a question—no second thoughts or hesitations. Two, they have no idea and take a guess. And three, they're absolutely sure they know the answer but can't fully articulate it.

This third and most excruciating experience is called the *tip-of-the-tongue* phenomenon. But why does this happen if memory retrieval is automatic?

Consider an example: You are asked the question, "Who was the first American to win the Tour de France?" There are a few Americans associated with the Tour de France, most notably Lance Armstrong. When you first hear the question, you might think about Armstrong, though you might also know that he was not the first American to win the race.

At this point, your facility in retrieving one name interferes with others that you *might* know about. In Chapter 2, we talked about memory as if it were a bunch of five-year-olds hoping to be picked for a prize and that each successful memory is retrieved both because it jumps higher than the others and because it pushes down the others effectively. A name that may not be very easy for you to access in the first place (in this instance, Greg LeMond, who actually was the first American to win the Tour de France), will be easily jostled, which creates the conditions for the tip-of-the-tongue phenomenon to occur.

In this situation, it is often useful to take some time away from the problem. Experts refer to this as an *incubation period.* Early research on problem solving suggested that this break might have allowed a mysterious subconscious process to find a solution for you. Implicit in this way of thinking about problem solving is the idea that your unconscious mind does its own Smart Thinking and somehow gets back to you with the right answer when it has solved your problem.

Although it would be nice if you could do Smart Thinking without even being aware of it, your unconscious mind is not that hardworking. Instead, when you take a break, you are generally allowing your memory to fall back toward its resting state. The five-year-olds who got picked as memories rejoin their friends. Those who got pushed down have a chance to get back up. This break allows you to return to the problem at a later time and retrieve new information that might be more helpful to problem solving.

For this break to be effective, it is important that you really avoid thinking about the problem in ways that would continue to keep the memories you retrieved active and actively pushing back competing memories. There are lots of ways to take this kind of break. One way is to work on something else for a while, so that you engage your mental resources in another task. Another possibility is to get away from working altogether and to exercise, go for a walk, or take a shower. These more relaxing breaks can aid Smart Thinking in two ways. First, because these tip-of-the-tongue states are stressful, your relaxing aids memory. Second, getting yourself away from the work environment is often a better way of keeping yourself from thinking about the unsolved problem (the white bear) than staying at work.

A Language for Smart Thinking

To change *what* you are thinking about, you need to change the description of the problem. There are many modes of description. Clearly, we often use words to describe problems. However, we can also draw pictures and form mental images. We can even imagine sounds. All of these modes of thinking can influence the way we think about a problem.

As an example of the way you can change your description of a mental image, try this case from a classic experiment:

> Imagine a capital letter D. Now, rotate the letter 90 degrees coun-
> terclockwise so that the flat side is on the bottom. Add to it a
> capital letter J and put that J at the base of the D. What have you got?

Most people who hear this description are able to recognize that they have formed a mental picture of a simple umbrella. In this case, I never mentioned umbrellas, so to be able to recognize what you have formed, you must have generated an image. This image then served as a cue to your memory to retrieve things that look like your image, and you were reminded of umbrellas.

Another important aspect of this example is that the mental image allowed you to be reminded of a word that described it. In this way, thinking about images can influence the language you use to describe a situation. That can also be a valuable part of Smart Thinking.

How do images differ from language? Quite a bit of research shows that some things are easy to describe using words and sentences, but others seem best described in pictures. It is particularly easy to describe objects and the properties of those objects with language. We have a rich vocabulary of nouns and adjectives that allows us to talk about what things look like. So, you might describe an object on a table as:

A large yellow plastic cup.

This simple description provides information about the size, color, and material of an object. We also have verbs that permit descriptions of actions involving people and objects. We might describe a simple scene by saying:

The dog lapped water from the blue plastic bowl.

In this example, we get information that the dog drank from the bowl as well as the way the dog did it (by lapping the water with her tongue).

Other information is harder to state effectively with language. It is often difficult to describe specific *spatial relationships*. You might be standing outside looking for a ball that someone has thrown. A friend sees the ball and tries to direct you to it. He might say,

It is to your left. No, a little more left. And about 10 feet from you. Well, maybe a little farther I guess. Keep going. A little to the right now. Look down.

You do have measurement systems for describing exact spatial relationships (like the measurements for angles and distance), but you do not usually use them in normal discussions. And even if you did use an exact measurement, the person you are talking to would not be able to find that exact spot without tools. Instead, you tend to guide people by starting with their current location and then giving them general relationships like *left*, *down*, or *farther*.

One way to talk about space more effectively is to draw an analogy to a familiar spatial image that people already know. People often use the clock face as a visual analogy to the world. You could tell your friend to look at two o'clock to find the ball.

Also, as discussed in Chapter 4, you have a smaller vocabulary for talking about *relationships between objects* than you do for talking about the objects themselves. You have words for basic relationships. You can say that one event *caused* another. You can talk about general relationships in time (one event *preceded* another) or in space (one object is *behind* another). But this relational vocabulary is not very expressive.

Finally, you are not very good at talking about many sensory aspects of what you perceive. It is quite difficult to talk about tastes and smells in any specific way. If you read reviews of wines, you see many terms like *oaky* or *fruity* or *with hints of earth* that are meant to describe tastes and smells. But it is difficult for even experts to agree on the meaning of these terms, and these experts spend many hours trying to learn to distinguish among these tastes and smells.

Similarly, while you can talk about general aspects of sound like pitch (high and low) and volume (loud and soft), it is difficult to provide a more specific description of sounds. Musicians also use terms like bright, dark, sharp, and rounded to describe the character of the tone of different instruments, but these terms are also quite broad.

The reason it is important to know the limitations of language is that when you encounter a problem that involves spatial relationships, relations among objects, or other sensory elements, then you should consider using other methods of description besides language to form cues to memory.

Using Diagrams as Descriptions

Given the limitations of language, when you get stuck on a problem you can consider ways to express elements of the problem *without using language* by using imagery. Diagrams and sketches are particularly useful to help describe and understand the facets of an issue that are hard to describe with language. This, in turn, promotes acquiring High-Quality Knowledge and creates good cues to memory to allow you to Apply Knowledge.

When describing a process, it is often useful to create a diagram that lays out the order of steps. You might be able to do the same thing only with words, but the diagram provides a way to illustrate repetitions of steps and choice points in a more compact way than you would with words.

For example, I can describe in words all the steps in a tennis game between a server and a receiver. The basic rule for a tennis game is easy to state. The first player to reach four points and to be ahead by two points is the winner of the game. Yet this simple description masks a number of steps that players have to go through to complete a game.

The game begins by having the players play a point. The winner gets a point added to her score. If no player has four or more

points, then they play another point and go through the same
procedure. If one player does have four or more points and is
ahead by at least two points, then that player wins. Otherwise,
another point is played and the same procedure is followed. Once
a player has four or more points, and is ahead by at least two
points, that player wins the game.

This same procedure can be described in a diagram like the
one below:

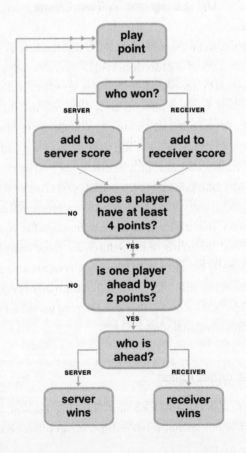

Diagrams like this are particularly effective at representing the ordering of steps in a procedure. When a procedure requires different sets of steps depending on some condition (like how many points have been scored), then it is easy to see the steps that need to be taken. In addition, when a procedure feeds back on itself so that you have to go back and repeat a previous step, it is also easy to follow the chain of steps. In this way, diagrams provide an excellent mode of description for tracing through a complicated procedure that may help you think about a situation in a different way.

Diagrams can be useful for causal understanding as well. Describing the steps of a procedure with a diagram helps uncover the gaps in your understanding. Missing steps in the description of a procedure become obvious in a diagram. In addition, the links between one box and another in a diagram are often places where there is a causal relationship between one step and another. Even this simple diagram of a tennis game makes clear that a player's point total goes up because that player has won a rally.

Once you have developed a diagram for a problem that you are trying to solve, that diagram can then influence what you retrieve from memory. Diagrams of procedures are more complete than what can usually be stated with language. They are also generally more abstract, because they do not contain many specific references to objects. As a result, they can be quite useful for supporting the retrieval of analogies.

THE POWER OF SKETCHES

Sketches are also valuable for Smart Thinking. Because it is difficult to talk about spatial relationships, it can often be useful to draw a picture of a solution to a problem. This can be particularly helpful when creating the design for some new object. You might be concerned about trying to use sketches in problem solving if you have never had any classes in drawing and are concerned about your artistic ability. Part of the power of sketches, though, lies in the difficulty of capturing a complete solution with a high degree of accuracy in a sketch.

In studies I did with my colleagues in mechanical engineering Kris Wood and Julie Linsey, we explored the role of sketches in group problem solving. The participants in this study were mechanical engineering students. They were asked to design a device for removing the shells from peanuts that could be used in a third world country. To make the design practical, it could not use electricity.

The groups that were most effective in these experiments were those that passed ideas around using a combination of words and sketches. The sketches allowed people to display the relationships among the parts of the objects, while the words were good for describing functions that were hard to draw. For example, one group wanted to soak the peanuts first to make the shells soft. It was easy to draw the water container, but hard to make clear that the peanuts had to soak for a while without being able to use words.

A surprising aspect of a sketch is that it may lead to unanticipated reminding. In one group, a person wanted to have the device powered by the wind, and so she drew a propeller for capturing wind energy. The sketch was quite rough, though, and it reminded another participant of a water turbine. So, he added onto the original sketch by drawing water flowing past the propeller/turbine. This unexpected result would have been unlikely to occur if the word *propeller* had been used. Because the drawing could serve as a cue to memory, though, a novel and unexpected addition to the design was added.

Finally, sketches are useful in the early stages of problem solving because they do not include many of the specific details that might be included in a prototype or model. New technologies have been developed that allow rapid prototyping in which an idea can be turned quickly into a real three-dimensional object. Psychologists Chris Schunn and Bo Christensen studied designers working on medical devices. They found groups that created prototypes too quickly got fixated on specific details of the prototype rather than focusing more broadly on the problem they were trying to solve. As a result, they focused the rest of their problem-solving efforts on fixing flaws in the prototype rather than ensuring that they had found the best solution to their problem. Groups that worked with sketches and preliminary drawings rather than prototypes were more likely to explore a wide range of possible solutions to their design problems.

USING GESTURES

Expressing relationships can also be assisted by making hand gestures. If you watch people make gestures when they speak, there are a few different ways that people use their arms and hands. Some gestures are just rhythmic. They keep time with the cadence of a person's speech. Some gestures are clearly meant to communicate. A person who says, "Look over there," and points is using this kind of communicative gesture.

Many gestures that people make function as much to help someone figure out how to say what they want to say as they do to communicate information to the listener. These gestures are particularly good at helping you to describe a relationship between the parts of a process that may be hard to describe with words alone. If you are talking about a process in which two components are combined together, you might start with your hands apart and bring them together while talking about combining the items. When talking about the speed and direction that something moves, you often make gestures that have a similar speed and direction. Even if your conversational partner isn't looking at you (like when you are talking on the phone), you still make these gestures because they help you think about the relations.

Children also use gestures to help them learn new concepts. They often make gestures that correspond to relationships they are learning before they can describe those relationships with words. When learning addition, children will look at equations on a page. They have to learn that the two numbers on the left side of the equation are combined to form the answer. Before they can describe that is what they are doing, many children will point to one number with each hand and then bring their hands together. Soon after starting to make these gestures, children learn to add numbers properly.

The gestures seem to function to give children a physical manifestation of the abstract relationship they are learning. The gestures allow the children to feel and see aspects of the relationship as they learn it.

The same technique can help you when you reach an impasse during problem solving. The best problem descriptions for retrieving analogies are ones that focus on relationships among the objects in the problem. If you are still working out these relationships, then gestures provide a way of making your growing understanding of the problem more concrete. Thus you should allow yourself to gesture as you redescribe the problem, which will help you find relations that may provide the basis for calling knowledge to mind.

The Takeaway

As counterintuitive as it may sound, memory retrieval is effortless. If your attempts to retrieve and use your knowledge induce a sweat, you're doing something wrong. And when retrieval does feel hard, that is an invitation to walk away from the problem for a while.

Your memory did not evolve to support an accurate playback of your life. Instead, it evolved to give you the information you are likely to need when you need it.

When you learn new information it becomes associated with the context in which you are learning. Using your knowledge effectively requires getting High-Quality Knowledge into your memory and then creating a context that is similar to the one in which it was created.

Because your ability to solve new problems depends on the quality of your knowledge, you have to maximize the value of the information you store in memory. Effective learning requires that you process deeply, explain things to yourself, and be active in your pursuit of knowledge. Effective learning is a marathon, not a sprint.

The key to solving problems is to recognize that when you get stuck you are not calling to mind knowledge you have that might help you solve the problem. If you have knowledge that will enable you to solve the problem, then you need to change the description of the problem to create new cues to memory that will bring new knowledge to mind. Use the power of proverbs, stories, and even jokes to capture the essence of the relational structure of the problem. Use images, diagrams, or gestures, especially when problems involve spatial or causal relationships. Each of those descriptions provides another cue to memory that may help retrieve useful facts for solving the problem.

SEVEN

Smart Thinking in Practice

Writing good summaries leads to
High-Quality Knowledge.

Get to know your Need for Closure.

Key steps generate new problem
descriptions and evaluate your solutions.

READING A BOOK ABOUT SMART THINKING IS A BIT
like reading a book about golf. A good golf book teaches
you the mechanics of a well-executed golf swing, gives you strategies for selecting clubs, and provides tips for the mind-set you
need to be successful on the course. This knowledge is helpful, but
it will not make you a better golfer by itself.

Ultimately, a golfer's game improves by *doing* rather than reading. The great golfers are the ones who put in their time on the
practice tee and the putting green. They turn their conceptual
knowledge of the game into Smart Habits that allow them to function at a high level as a matter of routine.

Smart Thinking also has to be learned by doing. Up to this point
in the book, I have explored the key elements of the formula for
Smart Thinking: Creating Smart Habits to acquire High-Quality
Knowledge and then Applying Knowledge. This chapter focuses

on how to create the thinking equivalent of the practice tee. There are two aims here: To provide structures you can use to guide you to making aspects of Smart Thinking a part of your daily life and to provide methods for recognizing when you have reached an impasse and ways to move forward.

Recommendations for Good Practice

Chapter 2 explored the factors that govern the creation of habits. Smart Habits form an association between the information in the world and an action so that you no longer need to make an explicit decision about the behavior you want to carry out in any given circumstance. Practice is structured to provide a consistent environment that is repeated so that the behavior you want will ultimately be done automatically.

Before we get started, though, I have two recommendations for creating steady improvement in your thinking.

First, don't try all of these suggestions at once. Every change in habits that you make creates an additional behavior you have to think about. If you try to institute too many changes at once, you will spend all of your time thinking about *how* you think and not so much time actually thinking.

Second, making changes in your physical environment will help you remember the new behaviors you are adding. By way of example, consider the problem facing supermarkets that are trying to cut down on the number of paper and plastic bags they use. Markets have sold reusable bags to customers hoping they would bring these bags with them, and many customers have purchased these bags because they recognize the value of using them. Unfortunately, many shoppers keep the reusable bags in the trunk of the car and often forget them until they're already in the store. To help solve this problem, supermarkets have put up signs throughout the parking lot to remind people to bring their bags into the store. While this may be effective to a degree, the best course is to *make your own changes*: Always write at the top of your grocery list, "Bags!" (and make sure you have that list in a place you can see it before you exit the car).

By adding elements to your environment that remind you of actions that you are supposed to perform, you are providing a framework or scaffold to support your new behaviors. Eventually, these actions will become habits that are directly associated with the environment in general, and the changes in your environment are no longer needed.

Finally, just as any good book about golf provides tips and drills for players of many different skill levels I will provide a number of recommendations at different levels so that you can tailor the suggestions for changing the way you think according to your current habits.

IMPROVING YOUR SUMMARIES

Creating High-Quality Knowledge starts by controlling what you remember about new situations. In Chapter 3, I talked about the importance of taking a few moments to *summarize an experience before moving to the next thing*.

If you are not already in the habit of making these summaries, the first thing you need to do is to structure your environment so that you generate summaries as a routine after reading a book or article, or attending a meeting or talk. Start carrying around a notebook or tablet. Write the word *Summary* on the cover. When you've completed the book or article or at the end of a meeting, write down the three (or so) main points.

Use technology to help you as well. Many smartphones and tablets have note-taking apps. Set up a notebook in one of those apps to store your summaries. These programs provide an easy and environmentally friendly way to increase the quality of your knowledge.

As you develop the habit to summarize the outcome of what you read or hear, start to pay attention to the *kinds* of information you tend to write down. By exploring the content of your summaries, you can help improve the quality of what you remember later.

When you attend a meeting, do you focus your summaries mostly on the follow-up steps *you* have to take? If so, then you may be missing other key developments that are being discussed. When you go to a meeting, bring your to-do list. If a new deadline, meeting, or task is given to you, write it down on that list immediately. Now you do not need to include it as part of your grand summary of the meeting because it is already part of your schedule.

Focus your summary on knowledge you will need for the long term. If your meeting summaries are focused mostly on information that will only be relevant for the next week, then there are probably long-term issues that you are not going to be able to remember later.

What about your summaries of lectures, books, and articles?

Learning about almost any body of knowledge is a little like meeting the family of a new romantic partner for the first time. You sit down to dinner, and the conversation around the table is hard to understand. The discussion refers to events that happened years ago and to people who are known to everyone at the table except you. Occasionally, someone reacts strongly to a comment or question in a way you do not expect. Clearly, that comment referred back to something that happened in the past that you do not know about. Over time, of course, you learn about the various family relationships and family secrets, and you even become a part of this long-running family conversation.

Similarly, any body of knowledge has been developing over a long period. You are stepping into a conversation that has been going on for a long time. You need to get to know the basic objects, events, and people that make up this area of knowledge, and to learn to make predictions about how new events will affect that area. Only after you have basic knowledge of objects and events can you then really begin to tease out the causal knowledge that explains why things happen.

Take history as a case in point. If you are learning about the history of a new region, you must find out about key people who figured in historical events. You are exposed to important events, and the dates of those events. You can then look at relationships between events and start to trace timelines. As your command of these general facts improves, you can also start to look at the variety of causal forces that influenced these events and even the controversies among historians about the factors that contributed to these events.

Your summaries of lectures, books, and articles will reflect that transition from basic knowledge to causal knowledge. Over time when learning about something new, your summaries should also reflect a transition from objects (and people) to events and situations to causal knowledge.

To ensure that you develop your knowledge, organize your

summaries around three elements: objects (people), events, and causal understanding. As an example, when I teach students to read psychology papers, I suggest that they describe the basic experimental procedure being used (a set of objects), the important pattern of data emerging from that study (an event), and the theory (or theories) supported by this pattern (a causal explanation). There are two key reasons for this suggestion. First, if you know these three elements about a paper you have read, then that knowledge will often help you to remember other details as well. Second, repeatedly answering the same three questions about papers develops the Smart Habit to look for this information whenever you read a paper.

These summaries also provide you with opportunities to identify potential shortfalls in the quality of your causal understanding of situations. In Chapter 4, I identified two aspects of causal knowledge that may create important limits: gaps and undefined terms.

Generating summaries is a helpful way of identifying gaps. When you reach the part of your summary in which you are describing your causal understanding of the situation, you are generating a self-explanation. Your summary is not likely to be a complete explanation of what you learned, but it does provide you with a chance to review your current causal understanding.

After writing out that summary, look over the words you used in your causal explanation. Some of the words may mask gaps in your causal knowledge because you understand them less well than you think. So, your summaries also provide a chance to find terms whose meanings are not obvious.

To illustrate this point, I return to the flush toilet example from

Chapter 4. When I first tried to generate an explanation for why most but not all of the water in the toilet bowl is sucked out, I realized that I had a gap in my knowledge. This gap resulted because the pipes that lead the water out of the toilet bowl are hidden from view.

After searching for explanations of the way toilets work, I found a description and diagram that illustrated the internal mechanism. The hole at the bottom of the toilet bowl leads to a pipe that rises to a hump and then falls and connects to pipes in the floor that take the waste from the toilet bowl away. This hump creates a siphon that pulls most of the water out of the tank. All that is left in the bowl afterward is an amount of water that rises to the height of the hump in the pipe.

When I first encountered this explanation, I was happy that I had filled a gap in my causal knowledge, and I wrote out a brief summary for myself. Later, though, I realized that the word *siphon* was a problem. I know what a siphon is. As a kid, I learned how to siphon rainwater out of window wells next to the basement of my house after big storms. However, when I read my summary I realized that I have no idea how a siphon actually works, I just know that once a flow of water begins in a siphon, additional water is sucked in behind it. Thus reading my summary enabled me to identify a gap in my knowledge caused by a term I did not truly understand. And that created an invitation to fill this new gap.

PRACTICING FOR IMPASSES

When you read a book about golf, many of the tips focus on methods for refining your swing. These suggestions are meant to be practiced at the driving range. Of course, the driving range provides perfect conditions. The tee box is flat, and there are no obstructions. The range is meant to allow you to produce the same swing repeatedly.

On a real golf course, the terrain is rarely as perfect as it is on a driving range. The ground may slope upward or downward. The turf may be overgrown, or there may be bare patches in the grass. The ground may be hard from a lack of rain. The expert player has to practice for all of these situations.

Similarly, practice for Smart Thinking requires good preparation for dealing with impasses. When you get stuck during problem solving, your natural inclination is to feel the frustration that comes with not knowing how to proceed. This section focuses on specific techniques for dealing with impasses.

The worst impasses are easy to recognize. They involve that broad frustrating feeling that you do not know how to proceed with problem solving. However, the most common kind of impasses is harder to detect.

This more subtle kind of impasse occurs when you focus only on solutions to problems you have tried in the past, even though those solutions may not have been successful. While you have what may appear to be a solution to your problem, it is not always satisfying. You then need to make a decision about whether to adopt that solution or to continue Applying Knowledge to the problem to find new possibilities.

Impasses and Need for Closure

To ensure that you consider enough possible solutions to be confident you have found a good one, start by getting to know yourself a bit better. Psychologist Arie Kruglanski at the University of Maryland suggests that people differ in their *need for closure*. People high in need for closure tend to like to finish their cognitive work quickly. They consider only a few alternatives when making choices. They select courses of action without extensive deliberations. People low in need for closure tend to consider many different alternatives and to deliberate much longer before acting.

Need for closure is about more than just wanting to think about options, though. It really has to do with wanting to be done with the deliberation process. Not long ago, I had the chance to watch two teens order ice cream at a local shop. One walked up, glanced at the list of available flavors, and ordered the Belgian chocolate. The other stared at the list for a few minutes and then asked to taste three of the flavors. He sampled each one carefully, and then got a pained look on his face. There wasn't much additional information to gather, he just didn't want to make a selection. The Mexican vanilla and cinnamon bun flavors were both appealing, and choosing one would mean forgoing the other. It was easier for him to continue thinking about flavors than to bring closure to the process and pick one.

What is your typical approach to problem solving? Reflect on the many choices you make. Do you typically like to finish the process of thinking and move on with taking action? Do you tend to be the sort of person who avoids reaching a final decision, pushing off a choice to the last minute? Do you fall somewhere in between?

Either of these extremes can pose a problem for Smart Thinking. People *very* high in need for closure will often settle too quickly on a solution. Retrieving good analogies from memory, though, requires some effort to generate the proper description of the problem. Thus the first solutions that people find are typically those that come from the same domain in which the problem is stated. Someone trying to find a way to make vacuums hold their suction longer might focus on finding new designs for the bags to make the filters less likely to clog. Only after realizing that these solutions are inadequate is someone likely to look for other descriptions of a problem that support Applying Knowledge from distant domains (like thinking about vacuums more abstractly as having to find a way to separate dirt from air).

Of course, it also becomes problematic if you generate endless numbers of possible solutions without ever selecting one. Smart Thinking requires both finding potential solutions and recognizing that they are going to be useful. People with a low need for closure avoid committing to a particular decision. For them, there is always the potential that there will be another option that will provide an even better solution to the problem. The danger with this approach is well characterized by the proverb "The perfect is the enemy of the good." Eventually, overthinking provides diminishing returns relative to acting.

Sometimes, it is helpful to find a way to get beyond the choice point. For the teen who had difficulty picking a flavor of ice cream, I eventually pulled out a coin and assigned Mexican vanilla to heads and cinnamon bun to tails. The flip came out heads. At that point, he realized he was disappointed it hadn't come up tails and ordered the cinnamon bun.

Learn your own tendencies to determine the kinds of impasses you encounter. If you are high in need for closure, then you need to focus on developing new strategies for finding alternative solutions to problems. If you are low in need for closure, then you need to improve your strategies for assessing the quality of your ideas to determine when it is time to adopt one of the solutions you have developed. The next two sections focus on these elements.

FINDING NEW SOLUTIONS

A key lesson of Chapter 6 is that the best way to find new solutions to problems is to change the way you describe them. Specifically, you want to pull analogies from memory that will help you bring knowledge from new domains to bear on the problem. Finding analogies requires generating descriptions of the problem that focus on the relations that form the essence of the problem.

When you are not satisfied with the quality of the solutions for a problem that you have found, take that as an invitation to redescribe the situation. There are a few basic questions that can be asked to start this process. To put these questions into context, think about how to solve the problem of cleaning a white shirt.

If you get stuck answering a question like this, start by trying to describe the whole situation carefully. How would you describe the problem to be solved when you have to clean a shirt?

Often, you assume that there is some kind of stain on the shirt. In this case the problem to be solved is to find a way to remove the stain from the shirt.

In general, it is helpful to write out the current problem statement so that you can ensure you are being clear about the assumptions you are making about the problem. So the first key step for finding new solutions is as follows:

1. **Write out a statement of the problem.** Once you write out the problem statement, decide whether you think it is really the problem you want to solve. Stain removal seems like a reasonable way of thinking about the problem of cleaning a shirt, though the problem itself is not really stated specifically enough to actually solve it. Instead, you need to explore the kinds of stains that can affect fabrics to determine how they might be removed. Different stains might need to be removed in different ways. You cannot begin to generate methods for stain removal until you identify specific types of stains and particular materials from which they need to be extracted. Thus the next step:

2. **Ensure your problem statement is specific enough to be solved.** After you have exhausted the solutions you create from your initial problem statement, you may still feel as though there are more possible solutions out there. At this point, return to the initial problem statement and think about the broader situation in which the problem is embedded. Once you consider the broader situation, you may discover that there are other ways of characterizing the problem.

When contemplating shirt cleaning, what is the broader situation? There is a shirt, there is a stain, but there is also an observer. Another way to describe the problem caused by a stain is that it takes a shirt that should look white, and it makes the observer see other colors on the shirt. If there were a way to prevent the observer from seeing the stain, then the shirt would appear to be white, even if the stain were still present on the fabric.

Indeed, that solution is the one adopted by fluorescent whiteners. Over time, many white fabrics appear yellow, because oils from skin and other contaminants stick to the fabric. Fluorescent whiteners absorb ultraviolet light in the environment and give off a faint blue glow. The human visual system is constructed around systems that place colors in opposition. In this system, blue and yellow light are opponents. When a fabric absorbs blue light, it appears yellow. The fluorescent whitener replaces some of the blue light and makes the fabric *appear* white. In this case, the contaminants are still attached to the fabric, but they cannot be seen, because they are being hidden by the blue glow coming from the fluorescent whitener.

More broadly, then, the third key step of the problem process is the following:

3. **Broaden the description by considering more of the situation.** After creating this broader description, you can try to categorize the problem based on the kinds of relational labels discussed in Chapter 6. In some cases, you may know a word that applies to the problem once you describe it. For example, fluorescent whiteners are acting as a *camouflage*. At times, there may be many ways to classify the same problem, and each may suggest a different solution to the problem.

Returning to the stain example, there are other ways to make it hard for people to see a stain, though not all of them may be applicable for white shirts. Carpeting for high-traffic areas in office buildings often uses a variety of colors in an irregular pattern. One reason for this color scheme is that many stains that could get into this carpeting will not be obvious because it becomes difficult to tell which colors are part of the carpet's color scheme and which are part of a stain. In this case, the solution can be classified as helping the stain to *hide in plain sight*.

More generally, then, the last key step for finding new solutions is this:

4. **Find one or more ways to classify the essence of the problem.** To help you with this kind of classification, start to gather lists of proverbs, story titles, and joke punch lines that you can use to describe problems and solution procedures. It can be hard to come up with good labels to classify problems on your own. When you hear a good joke, write it down. Look through lists of proverbs on the Internet and find some that express situations that you recognize. Bookmark those lists so that you can read through them when struggling with a new problem that defies solution.

ASSESSING SOLUTION QUALITY

How do you decide when to stop generating solutions to a problem? It might seem obvious to say that you stop generating solutions when you have solved the problem. To some degree that is true, but that assumes you know when the problem is solved.

It is unfortunate that a lot of the practice we get solving problems during our education involves problems that have known solutions. Math classes give problems that have a correct answer, and one of the key skills you are taught in math is how to check your answer to ensure that it is correct. Many tests in history, English, and science classes focus on factual knowledge like the dates of crucial events, the characters in classic books, and the tenets of important scientific theories. This knowledge is important, of course, but it means that your education gave you a lot of practice answering questions that have a known and easily verifiable answer.

The many examples of Smart Thinking we have discussed so far (such as those by James Dyson and Fiona Fairhurst) were aimed at problems whose solutions were harder to evaluate. In these cases, a key problem is that the proposed solution is a plan that could take a long time to implement. Dyson spent years perfecting the design of a vacuum-size industrial cyclone before it could be brought to market. Somehow, he had to decide that this idea warranted an investment of time and energy well before he knew that his idea would succeed.

Clearly, it is not possible to know in advance whether an idea will succeed. In this section, though, I focus on three issues that can improve your evaluation of ideas. First, I examine the role of confirmation bias in evaluations. Then, I explore the way that positive feelings can influence your judgments of the quality of ideas. Finally, I discuss the importance of evaluating a specific proposal for implementing the idea.

Confirmation Bias

When you start a new job, you are probably conservative in your social interactions with your new colleagues compared to your interactions with friends. With old friends, you can argue about politics, tell off-color jokes, and disclose sensitive personal facts. With new coworkers, though, you probably avoid discussions of politics, tell only the most sanitized jokes, and avoid lots of highly personal topics.

Over time, you may overhear jokes told by colleagues and get a sense of what type of humor is appropriate in your workplace. Chances are, though, that when you tell jokes of your own to the group, you will keep your topics well within the borders defined by the jokes you have heard told by your colleagues.

This very reasonable behavior is an example of a *confirmation bias*. That is, the first jokes you hear told by your colleagues form a belief about what is appropriate. When you tell a joke of your own, you are testing that belief. The safest way to test that belief is to stick within the range of what you already believe to be appropriate.

Of course, you could have tried it another way. Your initial belief might be that clean jokes are most appropriate. Scientific method says that the best way to test a belief is to find cases that could give you evidence against it. You could test your belief about appropriate jokes by telling a dirty joke in the office. That would certainly be effective at testing the belief, but if your belief was correct, your joke could get you fired. Because of these consequences, you normally behave in ways consistent with your beliefs, even if that means missing some opportunities.

Although a confirmation bias is a safe strategy in many social situations, it is not an effective way to evaluate new solutions to problems. When you are engaged in Smart Thinking, it is important to seek all of the ways that your current solution might not work. It is not pleasant to think through the limitations, but it is much less expensive to find the crucial flaw in an idea early on than to discover it after you begin to implement the solution.

That means that you have to develop the Smart Habit to ask what can go wrong with your solution. In particular, think about the assumptions you make about the future in order for your solution to be effective. It is important to determine whether those assumptions are realistic.

In the years before the financial crisis in 2008, many lenders enticed homeowners to borrow more money than they could afford to purchase a house. One way that lenders convinced skeptical homeowners that these mortgages were safe is that they pointed out that the loan could always be refinanced in the future. The key assumption here was that housing prices would continue to rise so that the value of the house would remain higher than the amount of money that was borrowed. Many homeowners did not question this assumption, and when home prices began to decline, they had to default on their loans. Those defaults ultimately put the financial industry into a tailspin.

It is not always easy to see the hidden assumptions that you are making when solving difficult problems. For this reason, it is useful to engage other people to help you during problem solving. When you think you have found a great solution to a hard problem, ask other people to help you evaluate it.

If other people raise objections to your idea, start by thinking carefully about those objections before deciding that they will not influence the success of your solution. You may ultimately decide that the objection is not significant, but you should start by taking it seriously. In addition, you may refine your idea by reflecting carefully on the objections other people raise. In this way, you can help yourself prepare for obstacles you may face in the future.

Positive Feelings

In Chapter 5, I told the story of Archimedes and his discovery of the law of displacement. It is important to remember that after stepping in the bath and realizing that the water spilled over the edge because it was moved aside by his body, he screamed "Eureka!" and ran down the street naked.

As this example reflects, solving a difficult problem feels good. In general, there is solid evidence that thinking quickly and successfully creates a positive mood. You probably feel good after having a great conversation with friends. One reason fast music tends to lift your mood is that you have to think quickly to follow along with it.

It is important to realize that the intense thinking that goes along with solving a difficult problem will contribute to your overall belief in the goodness of the solution you have developed. That is, the good mood generated by thinking colors your evaluation of the solution.

When you are trying to solve a difficult problem for which the solution will be difficult and expensive to implement, give yourself a cooling-off period before you make a final decision about the solution to pursue.

This issue is particularly important in group problem-solving situations. I have watched many groups work together to tackle a tough problem. When the groups work well, the ideas fly around the room. There is tremendous excitement and energy.

At the end of a session, groups often want closure. They want to leave the meeting feeling as if they had adopted a new direction. As tempting as it is to be able to say that you have adopted a course of action, it is important to realize that the excitement of the group problem-solving setting creates a positive mood that will make you feel rosier about the potential solution.

Rather than seeking closure after working hard on a problem and having an insight, rank order the potential solutions. This way, at the end of a problem-solving session, you have a statement of which solution you think is best. However, you should revisit the solutions again after several days have gone by. In this way, you can separate the mood created by the success of Smart Thinking from the quality of the idea itself. If you are still excited about the idea several days later, then that is a good sign the idea itself has a lot of merit.

Evaluating Specific Intentions

In general, good solutions to problems are ones that are specific enough to be turned into plans that can be carried out. The initial solution to a problem may be a general idea that ultimately needs to be implemented in some way. It is important to evaluate solutions at a level specific enough to envision how it would be carried. After all, even when an idea is contemplated specifically, it may still require significant effort to perfect. Even after understanding the structure of sharkskin, it took Fiona Fairhurst and her team at Speedo time to create artificial denticles in a fabric.

To make an idea specific enough to evaluate, it is important to create what New York University psychologist Peter Gollwitzer calls an *implementation intention*. A good implementation intention has three qualities. First, it describes the actions that need to be taken to carry out a plan. Second, it describes when and where those actions will be carried out. Third, it grapples realistically with the obstacles that may arise in trying to carry out the plan. Thinking carefully about obstacles is crucial for avoiding confirmation bias.

The psychologist and consultant Gary Klein has written extensively about the way experts make decisions. He points out that

many experts in complex areas like firefighting generate one possible solution at a time and then evaluate the solutions by forming
implementation intentions to determine whether they will work.

In his book *Sources of Power*, Klein tells the story of the leader
of an emergency rescue team who has to find a way to save a man
trapped in his car after it crashed into a concrete pillar holding up
an overpass. Initially, the rescue team wants to use a device called
the Jaws of Life that will widen the opening where the doors are
to get the man out. The leader notices that the posts on the car that
normally hold the roof on have snapped. He has heard about
other rescues in which teams have lifted the roof off the car rather
than prying open the doors, and he thinks that this solution might
work.

At this point, the leader creates an implementation intention.
He imagines the actions that the rescue team will have to take to
lift the roof. He goes through the steps they will have to take to get
the man out of the car. He checks to make sure there are enough
personnel to carry out the plan. Finally, he thinks through the
factors that could go wrong. After going through these three
steps, the rescue leader gives the go-ahead to lift off the roof.
The team tries this approach, and soon they have extracted the
injured man from his car.

In this case, not only did the rescue leader use the principles of
Smart Thinking to come up with a plan, but he formed a good
implementation intention before making the decision to proceed.

The Takeaway

Bringing Smart Thinking from the pages of this book into your life is a process. The key is to develop new Smart Habits that integrate these principles into real situations. In this chapter, we focused on some of the difficulties that may arise as you start to follow the formula for Smart Thinking more regularly.

To increase the quality of your knowledge, take a productive pause at the end of meetings, lectures, events, and books. Write a summary. Examine your summaries for evidence of gaps in your knowledge and terms whose meanings are not clear. Although you will have to think carefully about these summaries at first, eventually you will create Smart Habits to give good explanations of things to yourself.

Think about the way you naturally want to solve problems to become more aware of the hidden impasses in problem solving. If you are very high in need for closure, you may settle on a solution to a problem without exploring enough possibilities. If you are very low in need for closure, you may focus all of your efforts on generating possibilities and fail to reach a decision.

To generate high-quality ideas, it is also important to focus some effort on the questions you try to answer. At times, your first attempt to solve a problem may be stymied because you have not described the problem specifically enough to be able to solve it. After you have ensured that you have a specific problem to solve, you may want to see whether the description is too narrow. You may need to broaden the problem by considering more of the situation in which that problem is embedded. After you go through this exercise, you can apply the kinds of labels discussed in Chapter 5 to help you classify the essence of the problem.

Finally, work on improving the way you evaluate the solutions to problems. Often, having an insight that might help you solve a problem is only the beginning of a long process of implementing the idea. Thus you need to be sure that you are embarking on the right path before putting in lots of time and effort to work on a solution.

One barrier that may get in the way of finding good solutions is the natural tendency to ask questions to confirm that a solution is a good one rather than finding obstacles that may prevent the solution from working. A second factor that may make you overly optimistic about a solution you generate is that the Smart Thinking itself tends to put you in a positive mood. Make sure that the good feelings that arise from successful thinking do not affect your evaluation of the idea you generated. Finally, to do a good job of evaluating an idea, form a specific implementation intention to ensure that you have thought through the details of how you will put the idea into practice.

EIGHT

Creating a Culture of Smart

What is a Culture of Smart?

Cultures affect Smart Thinking.

Learn ten ways to create a Culture of Smart.

ADULTS RARELY WORK ALONE. MOST BUSINESSES
put teams together to solve hard problems. As a result, it
is not enough for one person in a group to do all the Smart Thinking. All of the members of a group need to participate.

Yet, we do not train people extensively to help make the people
around them smarter. The educational system is focused primarily on individual work and individual responsibility. Thus we do
not naturally think about how to create a Culture of Smart.

The focus of this chapter is expanding the scope of Smart
Thinking from individuals to organizations.

Your Social Network and a Culture of Smart

You are strongly influenced by the people around you. A 2007
study explored how people's weight was influenced by the weight

of the people around them. The data analyzed from a large number of individuals found that if you have friends who are overweight, then your chances of being overweight go up. There are lots of reasons why this might happen. One is the concept of *goal contagion*. Research suggests that you often adopt the goals and behaviors of the people around you. If people around you are overeating, you will want to overeat along with them. If people around you are exercising, you will want to exercise. Goal contagion is one way that your cognitive system helps you maintain a close relationship to the people around you.

Not only does your social network affect the foods you eat, it also influences your thinking habits. When a culture promotes behaviors that follow the principles in this book, then it becomes a Culture of Smart.

Cultures influence Smart Thinking both in obvious and subtle ways. Ultimately, the aim of this chapter is to provide specific suggestions you can apply to increase the amount of Smart Thinking by the people around you. To start this off, though, it is useful to think about the kinds of influences that a culture can have on your thinking.

At the most obvious level, cultures affect what activities you think are valuable to perform and which tasks are worthy of your effort. Learning new information is hard work. The people around you help signal whether you should engage in that hard work. When the management at a large company tells its employees that they should take training classes in areas that go beyond their core area of work, that is a clear signal that promotes Smart Thinking. In this way, an organizational culture can push people to learn about things that may help them in a task years later or may form the basis of an analogy in a new project.

Cultures also elevate the stature of the people who engage in activities that are valued by that culture. Many universities have been criticized because they give most of their honors and resources to faculty who are productive in their research regardless of the effectiveness of their teaching. In response, universities have started to give out high-profile teaching awards that are widely publicized within the university community and outside to send the signal that teaching is a core value.

However, some social structures do not always promote Smart Thinking. Wall Street has long given its respect (along with large bonuses) to people who generated significant revenues, regardless of the quality of the investments they were selling. In the years preceding the financial crisis in 2008, many people in the banking and mortgage industries took those bonuses as a signal that revenues were more important than integrity. This led many bond sellers and financial advisers to cut corners, and to sell financial products that they did not really understand. Other mortgage lenders engaged in outright fraud. Although many of these people made substantial profits in the short term, they did not develop the kind of High-Quality Knowledge that would allow them to predict the long-term ramifications of their actions.

An organization that wants to promote a Culture of Smart needs to seek out those employees who regularly engage in Smart Thinking and to give them positions of respect and leadership to send the explicit signal that Smart Thinking is crucial to the mission of the group. Companies are often quick to reward people who contribute to quarterly profits, but are less focused on rewarding employees who make everyone around them more effective.

All of these practices deliver clear and explicit messages about whether the core principles of Smart Thinking are highly valued by an organization. Many of the suggestions I present in the next section are things you can do explicitly to influence the value people place on the behaviors that lead to Smart Thinking.

Creating a Culture of Smart

Your own thought processes have been shaped by those of the people around you. Now that you have learned the formula for Smart Thinking, you can use it to influence others. In this way, you can help create a Culture of Smart. The rest of this chapter provides ten suggestions that aim to promote Smart Thinking in the groups and organizations where you live.

ENCOURAGE PEOPLE TO LEARN MORE ABOUT THINKING

In my workshops on thinking I ask participants to give me their expectations for what they hope to get out of it. I do so to get people to think about aspects of their lives that might be affected by learning to think better. Ultimately, the best way to use the principles of Smart Thinking regularly is to be aware of the many situations in which these principles might apply.

A crucial step for creating a Culture of Smart is to expand how much everyone knows about their own thinking.

This kind of encouragement is contagious. An old proverb says, "Give a man a fish and he eats for a day, teach him to fish and he eats for a lifetime." Recent research suggests that this proverb reflects the most effective way to give people advice. Often, people will ask for your opinion about an action they want to take or a product they want to buy. It is tempting in these situations to just tell them what you think is the best thing to do. However, people are far more likely to use your advice when you give them information that supports their own ability to make a choice. It is empowering to reach a decision on your own, so providing someone with knowledge relevant to the decision is a great way to be helpful.

Students in the honors program in psychology at the University of Texas do year-long research projects under the supervision of a member of the faculty. I work with these students to help them develop skills for reading and integrating primary research studies in psychology into their research. One of the main skills I show them is embodied in the Role of 3—finding the three main points of each article they read. I encourage them to take a moment after they complete each article and to summarize the three key points and write them down in a research notebook or on a sheet of paper that they can clip to their copy of an article.

If I gave the suggestion alone, students might follow it and improve their ability to acquire High-Quality Knowledge from the papers they read. However, I present this tip along with a discussion of some basic principles of memory similar to those described in Chapter 3. By providing a context for this suggestion, I am giving the students an opportunity to decide for themselves when they have encountered a new situation where the Role of 3 may apply.

CREATE AN ENVIRONMENT IN WHICH SMART HABITS THRIVE

Smart Habits are central to Smart Thinking. Because the environment governs a lot of habitual behavior, creating settings that support the elements of Smart Thinking will improve the quality of thinking throughout a group.

As discussed in Chapter 2, habits form whenever there is a consistent mapping between an action and the environment and when that action is repeated. Thus if you want to create Smart Habits in a group, ensure that the environment is structured so that habits can form. The layout of an office building should be organized to promote good habits. From setting up central locations for picking up office supplies or dropping off mail to establishing procedures to handling issues pertaining to the functioning of the building or creating procedures that are consistent (yet flexible) minimizes the amount of time that people spend looking for things or figuring out how to get things done. Every time those departments move or a procedure is changed, everyone in the company needs to spend time adjusting to this change—and establishing new habits.

This same principle applies to the way in which a company presents itself to consumers. One reason for the success of fast-food restaurants like McDonald's is that consumers can quickly develop habits for eating at restaurants because there is a consistent design across restaurants. The habits developed in one location can be used at any other location as well.

Disrupting habits can have a devastating influence on consumers' habits. When Microsoft changed the interface for its Office products from a menu-based system to the menu ribbon (introduced with Office 2007), surveys estimated that 80 percent of users responded negatively to the change. The reason for this negative reaction is that consumers who used earlier versions of Word, Excel, and PowerPoint had to change all of their habits of working with these products in order to adapt to the new system.

Consequently, many users elected not to upgrade their products rather than shift to the new system.

Thus companies need to ensure that they support habits both internally for their employees and externally for their customers.

BE OPEN TO IDEAS

The series of Harry Potter movies is enjoyable on a number of levels. Perhaps one of the greatest thrills of those movies for adults is watching a stellar cast of British actors take on the roles of the quirky characters of J. K. Rowling's novels.

There are a number of great scenes that take place in the classroom of Severus Snape, played with great relish by Alan Rickman. Snape, who teaches young witches and wizards to make potions, is a fearsome teacher. The students sit in the classroom with constant looks of alarm out of fear that they will make an error or say something that will lead to one of Snape's withering comments. Even those students who are supposed to be his favorites sit in the class rigid with terror.

As amusing as these scenes are in the movie, this setting is not ideal for Smart Thinking. People quickly adapt to the social environment. In a stressful work or academic setting, people will limit the contributions they are willing to make publicly because they are concerned about criticism. They may also be less likely to volunteer suggestions to their superiors when they feel those suggestions will be judged harshly. In the end, when people in a group close themselves off to new ideas, other members of that group quickly stop suggesting new options to consider.

To be clear, not every idea is a good one, and an important part of creating a Culture of Smart is for an organization to be able to distinguish between good ideas and bad ones. But the process of evaluating an idea requires trying that idea on for size first, before finding its flaws. Too often, though, members of a group have a negative reaction to an idea at first simply because the idea is new and unfamiliar.

Some people are open to new ideas as a central part of their personality. One of the core dimensions of personality is called *openness to experience*, and it reflects how likely someone is to embrace a new situation or idea. But even those people who are relatively low in openness can train themselves to consider new ideas deeply rather than rejecting them without due consideration.

A culture of openness has a remarkable effect on the people in it. Everyone feels more confident presenting new ideas when they believe that the general environment is supportive. When you grapple with someone's idea, you have honored her intellectual efforts, even if you ultimately have significant reservations about her suggestion.

To develop your own openness, think about the way you react to new suggestions. Do you find yourself thinking immediately about why a new idea is wrong? Do you feel a rising frustration when confronted with a suggestion that differs from your own? Do you resent someone for raising a new point, because it will slow down the process of reaching a decision?

When you find yourself becoming closed to experience, try two exercises. First, do not respond immediately. Give yourself the opportunity to think through a new idea before stating its flaws. Second, focus on the benefits of an idea and start your evaluations with a statement of the positives.

Demonstrating an openness to new ideas not only helps to foster an environment in which people present their best ideas but also helps the group to find the key benefits of a fresh approach. The germ of a great idea may be found in the positive elements of a proposal that may otherwise have deep flaws. Being open helps the group to capture the best components of each idea of the group's members.

EXPLAIN CLEARLY AND EXPLAIN OFTEN

A major barrier to High-Quality Knowledge is that many people do not explain things to themselves when learning. As a result, the illusion of explanatory depth can make people believe that they know more about the way things in the world work than they really do.

Once you have mastered the habit of self-explanation and avoided the pitfalls of the illusion of explanatory depth, you will be able to provide clear and comprehensible explanations that allow everyone to better understand information you present. However, it is equally important that others are encouraged to explain things for themselves—a Smart Habit that will not only help them to absorb High-Quality Knowledge but also help identify gaps in *your* knowledge—or in the way that you have communicated your ideas.

To support a Culture of Smart, though, it is important to react appropriately when people have difficulty providing good explanations when you ask for them. Just like you want to be open to new ideas expressed by group members, you want to react appropriately when someone cannot provide a good explanation. Gaps in someone else's knowledge are a problem for an organization, because those gaps limit people's effectiveness in problem solving. So, it is important that people treat any gaps they identify in their knowledge as invitations to learn more. Furthermore, as people come to expect that they will have to give explanations for their reasoning as a routine part of their presentations to others, they will generally do a better job of being prepared for giving those explanations.

CREATE DESIRABLE DIFFICULTIES

At some point, all of us are teachers; everyone has the chance to pass information on to the people around him. In those situations, you can improve the quality of what people learn by creating desirable difficulties.

Every year, the local Cub Scout troop holds its Pinewood Derby Race. The object of that event is for the scouts to build a race car out of a pine block. Part of the joy of the event is to create an artistic masterpiece that will stand out among all of the entrants. As each car is unveiled before the event, you can hear the kids chattering excitedly about who has the coolest car. But the real heart of the event is the race itself. The cars are lined up on a ramp. The starter throws a switch, and the cars roll down the track. The fastest car in each race advances until a final winner is determined.

Each scout had taken his own unique approach to the task. Some of the boys had clearly built their cars themselves. The designs had a certain blocky elegance. The wheels were not always completely aligned. These cars would roll and slide down the track in a manner befitting the handiwork of a second- or third-grader.

Other cars had a more professional appearance. One had the high-quality curves that could be achieved only with expensive power tools. The wheels were perfectly aligned. All the rough edges had been carefully sanded. These cars were works of art, to be sure, but also products that suggested the collaboration between parent and child had tilted in the direction of parental involvement.

Which is better? One could argue that the cars that were clearly built by parents had the edge. The boys whose cars flew down the track at amazing speeds were rewarded at the end of the night with handsome trophies. At the same time, the boys whose cars clunked slowly down the track could look with some pride on their own handiwork, even if it was not rewarded with hardware.

A closer look at the entrants in the race, though, revealed a third set of cars. A few of them had some real speed, but also had the childish design that reflected young hands. Talking with the parents of these boys, I discovered that the making of these cars reflected a real collaboration. These parents showed their children how to use the various tools in the garage. They taught their boys about friction and showed them how to sand the nails and wheels and how to ensure that the wheels were aligned when they were put on.

Building the cars was probably particularly frustrating for both parents and children. As a parent, it is often easier to just seize control of a complex process and let your child watch you perform an expert job. But true collaboration also creates desirable difficulties that lead to learning. The boys who really participated in creating a fast car learned a lot about physics and tools in the course of constructing their cars.

Every teaching situation should strive to create this kind of collaboration. A learner should not be left alone like the boys who built the cars themselves. Active teaching can provide a framework for learners to go beyond their existing knowledge, presenting new concepts and making key suggestions for improvements. At the same time, the learner has to do the bulk of the work for the lesson to be successful. Students will make mistakes, and often their execution will not reach the level of excellence of someone who has more expertise.

Russian psychologist Lev Vygotsky focused his work on the collaboration between teachers and students in learning. He argued that great teaching focuses on the *zone of proximal development*. That is, every student has a set of abilities and knowledge that are just out of reach. The ideal teacher creates a structure that helps the student to succeed at gaining that next skill and acquiring that next bit of knowledge without completely doing it for her.

Education should be like the scaffold that is used to help frame a new building. The teacher creates temporary structures that help the student learn something new. After the student has picked up the new knowledge, the scaffold can be removed, and the student can function effectively without it.

USE THE ROLE OF 3

Of all the suggestions that I can make in this book, the one that will have the fastest influence on the Smart Thinking of everyone around you is to respect the Role of 3—the principle that we remember roughly three things about every experience.

To help you develop the Smart Habit to use the Role of 3 regularly, whenever you are developing a presentation or running a meeting, use the following template to focus and organize your ideas:

TITLE OF PRESENTATION: ———————————

List three key ideas in the presentation:

1. ———————————————————————
   ———————————————————————

2. ———————————————————————
   ———————————————————————

3. ———————————————————————
   ———————————————————————

ORGANIZING THE PRESENTATION
Describe each key idea in one sentence:

1. ———————————————————————
   ———————————————————————

2. ———————————————————————
   ———————————————————————

3. ———————————————————————
   ———————————————————————

DEVELOP KEY IDEAS. FIND RELATIONSHIPS
1. **How is Idea 1 related to what people already know?**

   ———————————————————————
   ———————————————————————
   ———————————————————————

_____

_____

2. **How is Idea 2 related to what people already know, including Idea 1?**

_____

_____

_____

_____

_____

3. **How is Idea 3 related to what people already know, including Ideas 1 and 2?**

_____

_____

_____

_____

_____

**Three questions to help people remember
and self-explain ideas.**

1. _____

_____

2. _____

_____

3. _____

_____

Using this template will help you develop Smart Habits. Share this template with others in your organization to help spread good presentation skills and to focus presentations, meetings, and reports. These suggestions will guarantee that everyone comes away with a solid memory of what was discussed.

Finally, it is important to end each meeting and presentation with a review of the key elements that were discussed. This review will help create the Smart Habit that will solidify and clarify the memory of a situation. This practice will also provide encouragement for everyone to review meetings, presentations, books, articles, and reports for themselves before moving on to another activity.

NEGOTIATE MEANINGS

The core of High-Quality Knowledge is a good understanding of how things work—or causal knowledge. As discussed in Chapter 4, there are two key flaws in people's causal knowledge. One is that there may be gaps in what people know. The other is that people may use terms in their explanations whose meaning is not well understood. Poorly defined terms can flow quickly through an organization and provide an illusion of understanding of complex issues.

Legal scholar and linguist Lawrence Solan looks at the law as an example of the difficulty in figuring out the meaning of key terms. Lawmakers spend a lot of time setting up the wording of a particular statute to try to minimize the number of different ways that it might be interpreted. At the end of the process of writing a law, legislators typically hope that they have written a statute whose meaning is clear. As an example, he draws on a federal bribery statute that is written as follows:

> Whoever, directly or indirectly, corruptly gives, offers, or promises anything of value to any public official, with intent to influence any official act, shall be punished.

Even though the statute was written carefully, it turns out that it is difficult to develop agreement about the meaning of various terms. Who counts as a *public official*? What does it mean to do something *corruptly*? Which actions that an official takes are *official acts*?

In the legal system, these questions are answered through the sometimes long, arduous, and expensive appeals process. When someone is convicted of a crime based on a statute like this, lawyers for the defense may appeal the ruling by arguing that the statute does not apply to that particular case. For this federal statute, one appeal explored whether officials could be convicted of violating this statute if their salary came from federal funds, even though they were technically an employee of a state. These challenges ultimately help nail down the true meaning of the statute.

Thus even terms that are designed to be as clear as possible are open to interpretation. This issue becomes all the more important in groups. When companies generate mission statements and principles of operation, the words used have a significant influence on the future actions of the members of the organization. Yet, many of these terms are not presented with the level of attention to detail that goes into formulating laws.

To prevent fundamental disagreements in key terms from causing problems, it is crucial for people to really engage in a process of understanding what is being communicated. One key tool in negotiating the meaning of new terms is asking questions. When a term is not clear, we often try to understand it using the context in which it is used. For key terms in a causal explanation, though, asking direct questions about the meaning of a term provides a chance to be explicit about a concept that may ultimately play an important role in an organization's future decisions. These questions ultimately play the same role as the appeals and lawsuits in the court system. They provide a chance for the group to discuss and refine the meanings of terms. Without open communication, these disagreements will remain hidden.

These direct questions are important. People are often concerned about appearing ignorant in a conversation, and so they nod sagely when a new term is introduced. If you are an experienced member of an organization, though, you ought to understand what is being said. If a statement is made you do not understand, that is the speaker's fault, not yours.

Once, I was working with a large organization, and a senior executive gave a speech about the importance of doing more work with fewer resources in a difficult economy. This executive urged the group to spend the next year making the business more efficient by streamlining business processes. At first, everyone in the room nodded in agreement. It seemed to everyone that there was a clear set of marching orders. As the meeting went forward, the word *streamlining* was thrown around, and it seemed that the group was reaching a consensus that this was a plan to move forward.

At some point, though, one manager at a table in the back got a confused look on her face. She asked the group what they really meant by streamlining. The conversation stopped cold. It was immediately clear that nobody was sure what they were agreeing to do.

The discussion quickly turned to the meaning of *streamlining*. The term *streamlining* comes from engineering, and it refers to methods for reducing the forces of drag on moving objects. That is, streamlining is a term for making moving objects more efficient. Thus the group realized it was really being asked to become more efficient by making their business processes more efficient. After that, the group refocused the conversation to explore a more specific definition of efficiency that could actually be put into practice. Had they left the meeting just with the goal of streamlining the business, they would not actually have been any closer to achieving their goal.

In the end, asking questions about the meanings of terms is an effective way to guard against the illusion of understanding that can come from the use of vague terms within an organization. Negotiating the meaning of terms helps create a Culture of Smart.

DEVELOP LABELS TO AID ANALOGIES

My graduate mentor Dedre Gentner wrote a scientific paper a few years ago titled "Why We're So Smart" in which she argued that people—unlike any other species—have the ability to use language to create labels for things. Part of the power of labels is that they allow us to call discernibly different objects by the same name. For example, there are lots of things in the world that we call *trees*. As it turns out, many of the things we call trees are less related to each other than they are to other plants that we might call shrubs or flowers. What makes something a tree is that it is tall, has a woody stem, and provides shade. The two properties of being tall and providing shade are aspects of trees that relate them to people. So what really makes something a tree (as opposed to a bush or a shrub) is not some botanical property, but rather the relationship between those plants and humans. By using a label, we can group things together based on this relationship.

Labels get their power because they allow us to create groupings based on many different kinds of similarities. From the standpoint of Smart Thinking, many of the most powerful labels are ones that allow us to group together situations that are analogous. Chapter 5 discussed a number of ways to create labels for causal relations you may know. You might know a term like *collateral damage* that expresses the concept of unintended damage across different domains. Similarly, I described ways to use proverbs, story titles, and joke punch lines as ways to refer to situations that are analogous.

Perhaps the best part about labels is that they can be shared. By teaching other people in your organization the labels that you use to group together analogous items, you can use language to affect the way other people think. Linguist Dan Slobin has done research showing that the style of communication you adopt creates routines that lead you to think in a way that is consistent with that style of communication. Developing a sophisticated vocabulary with terms that refer to relationships and that group together analogous situations, then you help the people around you to develop the Smart Habit to look for new analogies.

DISCOURAGE MULTITASKING

Chronic multitasking places limits on Smart Thinking. But there is a lot you can do to help reduce the amount of multitasking in your environment. The most straightforward change is to ban multitasking in public settings in your group. I witnessed countless talks and meetings in which people are busily answering emails on smartphones and laptops while a speaker presents information.

Most groups tolerate this public display of multitasking with the occasional roll of the eye or shrug of the shoulders. Not every organization does. While a few heads of companies may defend the importance of multitasking in the modern world, more than one with whom I've worked does not allow anyone to bring a smartphone or laptop to high-level executive meetings. Everyone is expected to be mentally present for the conversation.

By removing all of the temptations for multitasking, these organizations are fostering a Culture of Smart. They are making clear that when an activity is truly important, it deserves everyone's full attention.

It is equally crucial to create the same respect for undivided attention in the workspaces of an organization. There are clearly times when multitasking is inevitable. At the beginning of each day, you might check your email, listen to your phone messages, and thumb through the snail mail from the previous day. At the same time you might check an organizational website to find out about new events that are going on that day. None of these tasks is particularly effortful, and there is no real harm in taking care of all of them at once.

When you are engaged in deep causal learning or putting in effort to redescribe a difficult problem, then multitasking can only hurt your chances of success. For these situations, your own Culture of Smart should have ways to eliminate multitasking. It could be as simple as encouraging people to shut off their email, IM, and smartphones. It could involve creating communal workspaces that are free of distractions or even encouraging people to sit outside to work uninterrupted.

In addition to the temptations technology creates that can lead to multitasking, the short-term goals created by technology can also provide a tempting oasis from the hard work that must be done to create High-Quality Knowledge. Most emails, phone calls, and texts create goals that can be achieved easily. A colleague sends you a short email asking for the phone number of someone, and you send it along. Your spouse sends you a text asking you to pick up milk on your way home. Your task list reminds you to download a few documents.

These short-term goals are easy to achieve and they provide an immediate sense of satisfaction or completion. In contrast, reading a complex and challenging paper can be effortful and frustrating. Those *desirable difficulties* are not always fun to work through, even if they do lead to good learning. Rather than buckling down and finishing that reading, it is easy to be diverted to your email or texts and get lost for a while taking care of short-term goals.

It is fine to take a break from an effortful task every once in a while but your learning experience will be diminished without sustained effort. You will not find ways to redescribe problems and Apply Your Knowledge. The more you avoid the difficult tasks you do, the less Smart Thinking you will do.

Multitasking is a behavior that is strongly influenced by the people around you. If you send clear signs that discourage multitasking, the people around you will think more carefully when they are tempted to do many things at once.

DON'T LET *I* STAND IN THE WAY OF *WE*

Creating a Culture of Smart seems on the surface to fly in the face of the strong individualism that is deeply ingrained in Western cultures. It is easy to caricature cultural differences, but one of the most pervasive elements of Western culture is its powerful celebration of individuals. From inventors (like Bell and Edison) to historical figures (from Alexander the Great to Churchill), we celebrate individuals and their influence on the world.

This culture of I is so deeply ingrained that we may not recognize the influence it has on our thinking. As I mentioned at the beginning of this chapter, our education system fosters competition for individual excellence. Schools grade students as individuals in classes. When teachers give group projects, parents worry that their children will not be adequately rewarded for their individual efforts and that one student's grades might suffer if the rest of the group does not do its share.

Yet most complex situations that require Smart Thinking happen in group settings. Companies may have strong leaders, but the best companies are the ones that have a strong corporate culture that prizes intelligence, flexibility, and innovation. Good managers are not necessarily those who have the most ideas but the ones whose groups are most effective. If a group works on a project and the project fails, then no individual in that group has succeeded.

Early in this book, I wrote about Johannes Kepler who was deeply interested in how the solar system worked. But he didn't get the right theory to explain the movement of the planets. Isaac Newton did get it right. Newton generated a theory in which bodies move unless forces act on them and the movement of the planets is governed by gravitational forces that are constantly pulling the planets toward the sun. But Newton knew that his success was due in part to the work of the scientists who came before him. "If I have seen farther," he said, "it is by standing on the shoulders of Giants."

Smart Thinking ultimately involves good thinking by individuals *and* by groups. Doing your part to create a Culture of Smart is a way of helping maximize your own success by improving the thinking abilities of the people around you. Ultimately, their Smart Thinking will also feed back to you. Even the flawed ideas of your colleagues can spur you to think about issues in a new way.

IN THE SUMMER OF 2005, I GOT A PHONE CALL FROM Craig Wynett, the head of the cognitive science group at Procter & Gamble (P&G). His job within the company was to bring insights from the sciences of the mind to the company broadly. Wynett's group had been introduced to some of my research and were particularly interested in understanding more about the psychology of analogy.

I mention Craig for two reasons. First, he really embodies many of the principles I describe in this book. Second, he has been instrumental at P&G for enhancing the Culture of Smart within that company.

Craig spent a number of years as a manager at P&G. He helped shepherd the Swiffer to market. The original Swiffer was the first product to incorporate a disposable pad at the end of a mop along with a bottle of cleaner that allows you to mop without having to pull out soap and a bucket. About $150-million worth of Swiffer products are sold each year. And that is only one of a number of successful brands that Craig worked on as a manager. Craig's contributions haven't stopped at the doors of P&G's offices. He has also played a crucial role as a coauthor with Mehmet Oz and Mike Roizen of the successful *You* series of books. Those books bring insights from the world of medicine to help people stay healthier, eat better, survive pregnancy successfully, and be more beautiful.

Of particular relevance to the concepts in this book, Craig is a strong adherent to the principles of Smart Thinking. He has an incredible need to know why things work. On one visit to the P&G offices, I found his desk littered with books and articles about waves and an electronics kit designed for kids where he was building simple oscillators. He had gotten interested in waves, and he wasn't going to give up until he was sure that he understood how they worked, even though it wasn't obvious at the time how that knowledge was going to solve any immediate problem.

In his role with the cognitive science group at P&G, he has amassed a significant library of important scientific titles in cognitive science, though other volumes cover a wide range of topics from how to build transmitter antennas to detailed works on evolutionary biology. He and his team gather in a conference room, spread out their materials, and work through difficult problems in how the mind works. The core idea in this group is that understanding how the mind works is the only route to making science-based suggestions about procedures within the company.

Originally, my conversations with Craig focused on helping them navigate the research literature. So whenever they were asked to help with a new project, they would call me for suggestions about other things to read or explanations about new concepts.

After a few years of these discussions, though, it also became clear that if other people in the company were going to accept recommendations about Smart Thinking, they also needed to know more about cognitive science. To help this process, P&G invited me to start teaching classes to their employees to help them understand more about the way they think.

What really impresses me about Procter & Gamble as an organization is their commitment to knowledge. They are happy to have their employees take a day away from their normal responsibilities to learn about thinking. The company certainly wants people to engage in effective procedures to get work done, but they really strive to have their employees understand why they work as they do. There is a true organizational commitment to developing and maintaining causal knowledge. In this way, the cognitive science group is contributing to a Culture of Smart at P&G.

As an example of how P&G uses the principles of Smart Thinking, consider the case of Tremor, a word-of-mouth marketing group that is a distinct organization within P&G. Word-of-mouth marketing involves giving people advertising messages that you would like them to pass along to their friends and neighbors to generate grassroots buzz about a product. Former CEO of Tremor Steve Knox wrote an article in *Advertising Age* about the company's formula for success.

Early on, Tremor did a great job of identifying people who were likely to be effective at passing messages. These people were the ones who had lots of connections within their community. They put together a panel of parents (mostly mothers) who were well connected to other parents and could make recommendations to them.

The problem was figuring out how to get those moms to talk about the products. Often, word-of-mouth marketing groups try to figure how to make it rewarding for people to pass messages. This mind-set comes from a comparison to typical advertising. The normal approach to advertising is to pay a radio or TV station to present a message or to pay to have an ad placed in a magazine or on a billboard. Similarly, the idea was to give some kind of incentive to members of a panel that would make it enticing to talk about a product with their friends. This incentive could be some kind of payment, but it might be access to exclusive information.

Tremor took a different approach. They redescribed the problem to focus on what makes people want to talk about things in general. They noticed that there are many situations that cause people to feel they simply must talk to someone else. A person who gets in a car accident will tell everyone the story of the accident for days afterward. As Knox points out in his article, after the pilot of a US Airways jet landed a crippled plane in the Hudson River without any loss of life, everyone wanted to talk about his incredible feat. These situations reflect that when events disrupt people's worldview, they need to talk about those events to create a coherent story about it. So they talk about it with everyone they know.

Using this as an analogy, Tremor set out to craft marketing messages about products that would cause similar disruptions in the way people think about products. The core of their business is to create messages about products that put people in a situation in which they simply have to talk about them.

To illustrate this approach, Knox points to a campaign they designed for a deodorant. Most people assume that the more active you are, the more you sweat, and as a result the more odor you cause. This particular deodorant had an ingredient that released additional scent when it got wet. They created a campaign around the idea "The more you move, the better you smell." This campaign challenged the way people normally think about deodorants, and led to a successful word-of-mouth campaign. Ultimately, more than 50,000 people left comments on the product's dedicated website.

Tremor succeeded in transforming its business by adopting an innovative approach to getting consumers to want to talk about products.

And that is Smart Thinking!

ACKNOWLEDGMENTS

Without that phone call from Craig Wynett, my work would not have taken off in the direction it has. I was struggling to find a way to bring cognitive science to a broader community, and he helped me find the way. The rest of the cognitive science group at P&G has also affected the shape of this book, including Pete Foley, Dan Young, Faye Blum, Evan Mathis, and Mike Ball.

Thanks to Mehmet Oz for his invaluable advice about book writing and navigating the publishing world.

A number of other colleagues and friends have made comments that have influenced this book, often without knowing it. They include Sian Beilock, Bob Dye, Dedre Gentner, Micah Goldwater, Jeff Lowenstein, Steve Knox, Brad Love, Todd Maddox, Viorica Marian, Doug Medin, Ross Otto, and Brian Ross.

I am grateful to the IC2 Institute at the University of Texas for a fellowship that supports my research.

Giles Anderson, my fantastic agent, has helped make this book better from the moment he first looked at it. I'm grateful that he stumbled on my blog for *Psychology Today*.

John Duff at Perigee lent his Midas touch to my prose. The book is much clearer for his hard work. Candace B. Levy provided a careful and conscientious copyedit, and Lisa Amoroso gave the book its stunning cover design.

Finally, I could not have finished this book without Leora Orent, who didn't want the book dedicated to her, even though it should be.

REFERENCES

1. WHAT IS SMART THINKING?

Smart is still normal thinking

Weisberg, R. W. (1993). *Creativity: Beyond the Myth of Genius.* New York: Freeman.

Chess expertise

Bilalic, M., McLeod, P., and Gobet, F. (2009). Specialization Effect and Its Influence on Memory and Problem Solving in Expert Chess Players. *Cognitive Science* 33: 1117–1143.

A few approaches to intelligence

Gardner, H. (1999). *Intelligence Reframed: Multiple Intelligences for the 21st Century.* New York: Basic Books.

Sternberg, R. J. (1985). *Beyond IQ: A Triarchic Theory of Human Intelligence.* New York: Cambridge University Press.

Evidence for thinking that being smart is a skill not a talent

Dweck, C. (2006). *Mindset.* New York: Random House.

2. CREATING SMART HABITS AND CHANGING BEHAVIOR

QWERTY and Dvorak keyboards

Diamond, J. (1997). The Curse of QWERTY. *Discover*, April: http://discover magazine.com/1997/apr/thecurseofqwerty1099.

Important papers on the development of habits

Logan, G. D. (2002). An Instance Theory of Attention and Memory. *Psychological Review* 109 (2): 376–400.

Logan, G. D. (1988). Toward an Instance Theory of Automaticity. *Psychological Review* 95: 492–527.

Schneider, W., and Shiffrin, R. M. (1977). Controlled and Automatic Human Information Processing: 1. Detection, Search, and Attention. *Psychological Review* 84 (1): 1–66.

Shiffrin, R. M., and Schneider, W. (1977). Controlled and Automatic Human Information Processing: 2. Perceptual Learning, Automatic Attending, and a General Theory. *Psychological Review* 84: 127–190.

Wood, W., and Neal, D. T. (2007). A New Look at Habits and the Habit-Goal Interface. *Psychological Review* 1114 (4): 843–863.

Research on habit learning and sleep

Walker, M. P., Brakefield, T., Morgan, A., et al. (2002). Practice with Sleep Makes Perfect: Sleep-Dependent Motor Skill Learning. *Neuron* 35: 205–211.

Walker, M. P., and Stickgold, R. (2006). Sleep, Memory, and Plasticity. *Annual Review of Psychology* 57: 139–166.

3. PROMOTING QUALITY LEARNING BY KNOWING YOUR LIMITS

Research on limits of attention

Pashler, H. E. (1998). *The Psychology of Attention*. Cambridge: MIT Press.

Vision, perception, and the influence of top-down information on perception

Hayhoe, M., and Ballard, D. (2005). Eye Movements in Natural Behavior. *Trends in Cognitive Sciences* 9 (4): 188–194.

Sekuler, R., and Blake, R. (1994). *Perception* (3rd ed.). New York: McGraw-Hill.

An introduction to research on thinking

Medin, D. L., Ross, B. H., and Markman, A. B. (2005). *Cognitive Psychology* (4th ed.). New York: Wiley.

Research on working memory

Baddeley, A. D. (2007). *Working Memory, Thought, and Action*. New York: Oxford University Press.

The structure of memory

Collins, A. M., and Loftus, E. F. (1975). A Spreading-Activation Theory of Semantic Priming. *Psychological Review* 82 (6): 407–428.

Collins, A. M., and Quillian, M. R. (1972). How to Make a Language User. In E. Tulving and W. Donaldson (eds.), *Organization of Memory* (pp. 309–351). New York: Academic Press.

Markman, A. B. (1999). *Knowledge Representation*. Mahwah, NJ: Erlbaum.

Tulving, E. (1983). *Elements of Episodic Memory*. New York: Oxford University Press.

Saying things out loud helps you remember them later

MacLeod, C. M., Gopie, N., Hourihan, K. L., et al. (2010). The Production Effect: Delineation of a Phenomenon. *Journal of Experimental Psychology: Learning, Memory, and Cognition* 36 (3): 671–685.

4. UNDERSTANDING HOW THINGS WORK

Johannes Kepler and his causal thinking

Gentner, D., Brem, S., Ferguson, R., et al. (1997a). Conceptual Change Via Analogical Reasoning: A Case Study of Johannes Kepler. *Journal of the Learning Sciences* 6 (1): 3–40.

Gentner, D., Brem, S., Ferguson, R., et al. (1997b). Analogy and Creativity in the Works of Johannes Kepler. In T. B. Ward, S. M. Smith, and J. Vaid (eds.), *Creative Thought: An Investigation of Conceptual Structures and Processes* (pp. 403–459). Washington, DC: American Psychological Association.

Differences between apes and humans in reasoning about causes and why it matters

Povinelli, D. J. (2000). *Folk Physics for Apes*. New York: Oxford University Press.

Tomasello, M. (1999). *The Cultural Origins of Human Cognition*. Cambridge: Harvard University Press.

Studies of explanation and the illusion of explanatory depth

Keil, F. C., and Wilson, R. A. (eds.) (2000). *Explanation and Cognition*. Cambridge: MIT Press.

Rosenblit, L., and Keil, F. C. (2002). The Misunderstood Limits of Folk Science: An Illusion of Explanatory Depth. *Cognitive Science* 26: 521–562.

The importance of self-explanation

Chi, M. T. H., Bassok, M., Lewis, M. W., et al. (1989). Self-Explanations: How Students Study and Use Examples in Learning to Solve Problems. *Cognitive Science* 13: 145–182.

Chi, M. T. H., and VanLehn, K. A. (1991). The Content of Physics Self-Explanations. *Journal of the Learning Sciences* 1 (1): 69–105.

5. MAKING COMPARISONS AND APPLYING YOUR KNOWLEDGE

The basics of similarity comparison

Gentner, D., and Markman, A. B. (1997). Structural Alignment in Analogy and Similarity. *American Psychologist* 52 (1): 45–56.

Markman, A. B., and Gentner, D. (1993). Splitting the differences: A Structural Alignment View of Similarity. *Journal of Memory and Language* 32 (4): 517–535.

Analogy

Gentner, D. (1983). Structure-Mapping: A Theoretical Framework for Analogy. *Cognitive Science* 7: 155–170.

Hesse, M. B. (1966). *Models and Analogies in Science*. Notre Dame, IN: University of Notre Dame Press.

Analogical inference

Clement, C. A., and Gentner, D. (1991). Systematicity as a Selection Constraint in Analogical Mapping. *Cognitive Science* 15: 89–132.

Markman, A. B. (1997). Constraints on Analogical Inference. *Cognitive Science* 21 (4): 373–418.

Analogy and communication

Moreau, C. P., Markman, A. B., and Lehman, D. R. (2001). 'What Is It?' Categorization Flexibility and Consumers' Responses to Really New Products. *Journal of Consumer Research* 27: 489–498.

Analogical problem solving

Clement, C. A., Mawby, R., and Giles, D. E. (1994). The Effects of Manifest Relational Similarity on Analog Retrieval. *Journal of Memory and Language* 33: 396–420.

Gick, M. L., and Holyoak, K. J. (1980). Analogical Problem Solving. *Cognitive Psychology* 12: 306–355.

Gick, M. L., and Holyoak, K. J. (1983). Schema Induction and Analogical Transfer. *Cognitive Psychology* 15 (1): 1–38.

Holyoak, K. J., and Koh, K. (1987). Surface and Structural Similarity in Analogical Transfer. *Memory and Cognition* 15 (4): 332–340.

6. MAXIMIZING MEMORY EFFECTIVENESS

Auguste Rodin

Elsen, A. E., Jameson, R. F., Barryte, B., and Wing, F. (2003). *Rodin's Art: The Rodin Collection of the Iris and Gerald Cantor Center of Visual Arts at Stanford University*. New York: Oxford University Press.

Flow

Csikszentmihalyi, M. (2008). *Flow*. New York: Harper Perennial.

The Mozart effect

Chabris, C. F. (1999). Prelude or Requiem for the "Mozart effect"? *Nature* 400: 826–827.

Rauscher, F. H., Shaw, G. L., and Ky, K. N. (1995). Listening to Mozart Enhances Spatial-Temporal Reasoning: Toward a Neurophysiological Basis. *Neuroscience Letters* 185: 44–47.

The core principle of memory

Tulving, E. (1983). *Elements of Episodic Memory*. New York: Oxford University Press.

Tulving, E., and Thomson, D. M. (1973). Encoding Specificity and Retrieval Processes in Episodic Memory. *Psychological Review* 80: 352–373.

Demonstration of the effects of context on memory

Godden, D. R., and Baddeley, A. D. (1975). Context Dependent Memory in Two Natural Environments: On Land and Under Water. *British Journal of Psychology* 66: 325–332.

Memory and college lectures

Bjork, R. A. (1994). Memory and Metamemory Considerations in the Training of Human Beings. In J. Metcalfe and A. P. Shimamura (eds.), *Metacognition* (pp. 185–206). Cambridge: MIT Press.

Reinterpreting objects in mental imagery

Finke, R. A., Pinker, S., and Farah, M. J. (1989). Reinterpreting Visual Patterns in Mental Imagery. *Cognitive Science* 13: 51–78.

Language for talking about space and relations

Gentner, D. (2003). Why We're So Smart. In D. Gentner and S. Goldin-Meadow (eds.), *Language in Mind* (pp. 195–236). Cambridge: MIT Press.

Newcombe, N. S., and Huttenlocher, J. (2000). *Making Space*. Cambridge: MIT Press.

Sieck, W. R., Quinn, C. N., and Schooler, J. W. (1999). Justification Effects on the Judgment of Analogy. *Memory and Cognition* 27 (5): 844–855.

The usefulness of diagrams, sketches, and gestures

Cheng, P. C. H. (2002). Electrifying Diagrams for Learning: Principles for Complex Representational Systems. *Cognitive Science* 26 (6): 685–736.

Goldin-Meadow, S., Wagner Cook, S., and Mitchell, Z. A. (2009). Gesturing Gives Children New Ideas About Math. *Psychological Science* 20 (3): 267–272.

Hegarty, M., Meyer, B., and Narayanan, N. H. (eds.) (2002). *Diagrammatic Representation and Inference*. Berlin: Springer-Verlag.

Linsey, J. S., Clauss, E. F., Kurtoglu, T., et al. (in press). An Experimental Study of Group Idea Generation Techniques: Understanding the Roles of Idea Representation and Viewing Methods. *Journal of Mechanical Design*.

Tip-of-the-tongue states

Schwartz, B. L., and Smith, S. M. (1997). The Retrieval of Related Information Influences Top-of-the-Tongue States. *Journal of Memory and Language* 36 (1): 68–86.

The difficulty with using models in complex problem solving

Christensen, B. T., and Schunn, C. D. (2007). The Relationship of Analogical Distance to Analogical Function and Pre-inventive Structure: The Case of Engineering Design. *Memory and Cognition* 35 (1): 29–38.

7. SMART THINKING IN PRACTICE

Need for closure

Kruglanski, A. W. (1996). A Motivated Gatekeeper of Our Minds: Need for Closure Effects on Interpersonal and Group Processes. In R. M. Sorrentino and E. T. Higgins (eds.), *Handbook of Motivation and Cognition: Foundations of Social Behavior* (Vol. 3, pp. 465–496). New York: Guilford.

Kruglanski, A. W., and Webster, D. M. (1996). Motivated Closing of the Mind: "Seizing" and "Freezing." *Psychological Review* 103 (2): 263–283.

Confirmation bias

Klayman, J., and Ha, Y. (1987). Confirmation Disconfirmation and Information in Hypothesis Testing. *Psychological Review* 94 (2): 211–228.

Koehler, J. J. (1993). The Influence of Prior Beliefs on Scientific Judgments of Evidence Quality. *Organizational Behavior and Human Decision Processes* 56: 28–55.

Mood and speed of thinking

Pronin, E., and Jacobs, E. (2008). Thought Speed, Mood, and the Experience of Mental Motion. *Perspectives on Psychological Science* 3 (6): 461–485.

Demonstrations that background emotions affect what seem to be unrelated judgments

Schwartz, N., and Clore, G. L. (1983). Mood, Misattribution, and Judgments of Well-Being: Informative and Directive Functions of Affective States. *Journal of Personality and Social Psychology* 45 (3): 513–523.

Implementation intentions

Gollwitzer, P. (1999). Implementation Intentions: Strong Effects of Simple Plans. *American Psychologist* 54: 493–503.

Expert decision making

Klein, G. (2000). *Sources of Power*. Cambridge: MIT Press.

8. CREATING A CULTURE OF SMART

Analyses of social networks

Christakis, N. A., and Fowler, J. S. (2007). The Spread of Obesity in a Large Social Network over 32 Years. *New England Journal of Medicine* 357: 370–379.

The financial crisis of 2008

Lewis, M. (2010). *The Big Short: Inside the Doomsday Machine*. New York: Norton.

Effects of goals on thinking

Aarts, H., Gollwitzer, P. M., and Hassin, R. R. (2004). Goal Contagion: Perceiving Is for Pursuing. *Journal of Personality and Social Psychology* 87 (1): 23–37.

Advice giving

Dalal, R. S., and Bonaccio, S. (2010). What Types of Advice Do Decision-Makers Prefer? *Organizational Behavior and Human Decision Processes* 112 (1): 11–23.

Mathematical proof I studied in my first seminar

Minsky, M. L., and Papert, S. A. (1988). *Perceptrons* (2nd ed.). Cambridge: MIT Press.

Teaching and culture

Vygotsky, L. (1986). *Thought and Language*. Cambridge: MIT Press.

Language and culture

Tomasello, M. (1999). *The Cultural Origins of Human Cognition*. Cambridge: Harvard University Press.

Influences of language on thought

Slobin, D. I. (1996). From "Thought and Language" to "Thinking for Speaking." In J. J. Gumperz and S. C. Levinson (eds.), *Rethinking Linguistic Relativity* (pp. 70–96). New York: Cambridge University Press.

Determining the meanings of words in the legal system

Solan, L. M. (2001). Why Laws Work Pretty Well, but Not Great: Words and Rules in Legal Interpretation. *Law and Social Inquiry* 26: 243–270.

Differences between eastern and western culture in the degree of individualism

Markus, H. R., and Kitayama, S. (1991). Culture and the Self: Implications for Cognition, Emotion, and Motivation. *Psychological Review* 98 (2): 224–253.

Nisbett, R. E., Peng, K., Choi, I., and Norenzayan, A. (2001). Culture and Systems of Thought: Holistic Versus Analytic Cognition. *Psychological Review* 108 (2): 291–310.

The role of symbols in human intelligence

Gentner, D. (2003). Why We're So Smart. In D. Gentner and S. Goldin-Meadow (eds.), *Language in Mind* (pp. 195–236). Cambridge: MIT Press.

Evolution of technology

Basalla, G. (1988). *The Evolution of Technology*. Cambridge: Cambridge University Press.

EPILOGUE

Knox, S. (2010). Why Effective Word-of-Mouth Disrupts Schemas. *Advertising Age*, January 25, 2010.

INDEX

Page numbers in **bold** indicate tables; those in *italics* indicate figures.

comparisons (*cont.*)
  reusing old knowledge in new
    situations, 122–23, 124–25
  similarities, finding, 125–33
  spatial relationships and, 124
  systematic (being) about choices,
    134
  time relationships and, 124
  unique nonalignable properties,
    133, 153
  See also analogies; Smart Thinking
complete explanations, 112–13, 119
computer vs. human memory, 69–70
conceptual information, 64
conceptual mappings, Smart
  Habits, 34
confirmation bias, 199–201
connections among knowledge,
  70–71, 74, 75, 82, 83–84, 87, 166, 169
consistent mapping, Smart Habits,
  33–35, 41, 42, 48, 54, 55
construal level, 110–12
content vs. abstract reasoning, 7
context and memory, 159–61, 167,
  168–69, 183, 195
continuity editors, 59–60
core thinking, comparisons, 130–31
cramming and studying, 168
cravings, 48, 51
crocheting, 50–51
crown of gold, 129–30
Csikszentmihalyi, Mihaly, 156
Cub Scouts, 216–17
Culture of Smart, 207–29
  active teaching, 217–18
  analogies and, 149–52, 154, 206,
    224–25
  Applying Knowledge and, 227
  casual knowledge and, 118, 119
  desirable difficulties, 165–66,
    216–18, 227
  explaining clearly and often,
    215–16
  goal contagion, 208
  High-Quality Knowledge and, 209,
    211, 215, 221, 227
  ideas, being open to, 213–15

I vs. *We*, 228–29
labels for categories of analogies,
  149–52, 154, 206, 224–25
learning quality and, 81, 84, 85, 87
multitasking, discouraging, 79–80,
  225–27
negotiate meanings, 221–24
openness culture, 213–15
questions to clarify meaning,
  223–24
Role of 3 and, 211, 218–21, **219–20**
Smart Habits and, 211–13, 215, 218,
  219, 225
Smart Thinking and, 18, 24
social network and, 207–10
stature of people and cultures, 209
thinking, learning about, 210–11
value of Smart Thinking in
  organization, 208–10
zone of proximal development,
  218
See also Smart Thinking
cyclone vacuums, 1–2, 3, 5, 8–10, 13,
  96, 97, 108, 110, 114, 199

Dante, 155
deep thinking, 164–65
de Mestral, George, 17, 24
denticles, 2
describing problems. *See* redescribing
  strategy
desirable difficulties, Culture of
  Smart, 165–66, 216–18, 227
diagrams, redescribing strategy,
  177–81, *178*, 184
dieting, 46, 47–48
differences, comparisons, 126, 127–28,
  130, 131, 132–33
digital cameras, 140
digital recorders, 81
Disney World, 36
Displacement, Law of, 129–30, 201–2
disruptions and Smart Habits, 39, 42,
  49, 50, 56, 212–13
distinctiveness of memory, habits,
  36–38
Divine Comedy, The (Dante), 155